THE NELSO

PICTURE
DICTIONARY

Name: _____

Age: _____

Address: _____

_____

_____

_____

_____

_____

JULIE ASHWORTH ■ JOHN CLARK

Nelson

Thomas Nelson and Sons Ltd
Nelson House Mayfield Road
Walton-on-Thames Surrey
KT12 5PL UK

51 York Place
Edinburgh
EH1 3JD UK

Thomas Nelson (Hong Kong) Ltd
Toppan Building 10/F
22A Westlands Road
Quarry Bay Hong Kong

© Julie Ashworth and John Clark 1993

First published by Thomas Nelson and Sons Ltd 1993
ISBN 0-17-556452 3
NPN 9 8 7 6 5 4 3 2 1

Printed in Hong Kong.

Acknowledgements

The authors and publishers would like to thank:
John Blundall and Cannon Hill Puppet Theatre for the use
of the puppets and masks on pages 16 and 17;
Childrens World, Crown Point Retail Park, Leeds, and
Sportstime, Arndale Centre, Leeds for the loan of toys and
equipment on pages 10 and 11; all the staff at Rodley
Studios for their help and care with the photographic work.

Design: Julie Ashworth

Photos: Anton Stark at Rodley Studios, Leeds (Tel: 0532
557272).

Illustrations: Julie Ashworth (pages 6, 8, 9, 20, 21, 40, 41, 42,
44, 45, 56, 57, 62); Rowan Barnes-Murphy (pages 24, 36,
37); Jerry Collins (pages 29, 57, 64); Andy Cooke (pages 25,
60, 61); Phil Dobson (pages 34, 46, 47, 48, 49); John Gosler
(page 63); David Parkins (pages 18, 19, 38, 39, 54, 55, 58,
59); Valeria Petrone (52, 53); Marie José Sacré (30, 31, 32,
33); Pippa Sampson (pages 12, 14, 22, 23, 50, 51); Peter
Schrank (pages 11, 28, 29, 30).

Note: Page 36-37
Monopoly is a registered trademark of Parker Brothers,
division of Tonks Corporation, Beverley 01915, USA used
under licence by Waddingtons Games Ltd. All rights
reserved. Cluedo is a registered trademark of Waddingtons
Games Ltd. The Beano is the copyright of D.C. Thomson &
Co. Ltd.

Introduction

Le Nelson Picture Dictionary est conçu pour être utilisé en classe ou à la maison. La présence d'une liste bilingue (anglais/français, français/anglais) permet l'utilisation du dictionnaire par ceux qui possédent peu ou pas l'anglais.

L'ouvrage est divisé en deux parties. La première est un dictionnaire en couleur illustré. Les mots sont classés par ordre alphabétique et rassemblés par thèmes. La seconde partie est une liste bilingue qui recense tous les mots du dictionnaire. Les mots y sont présentés par ordre alphabétique en anglais, accompagnés de leur traduction en français. Un renvoi est fait aux pages qui mentionnent le mot en première partie du dictionnaire. Une deuxième liste propose les mots en français suivis de leur traduction an anglais.

Comment utiliser ce dictionnaire

Pour trouver la signification d'un mot anglais ...

Si vous voulez savoir ce que le mot *skirt* veut dire, reportez vous à la lettre *s* dans la liste anglais/français à la fin du livre. A côté de mot, vous trouverez la traduction en français ainsi que la page où figure le mot.

Comment se dit tel ou tel mot en anglais ...

Si vous voulez trouver le mot anglais pour 'jupe', cherchez le mot à la lettre *j* dans la liste français/anglais à la fin du livre. Vous trouverez en face le mot anglais *skirt* suivi du numéro de la page sur laquelle figure le mot.

Ou bien encore ...

Consultez la table des matières (p 4/5) et recherchez dans la rubrique concernée, dans le cas présent, la rubrique CLOTHES (vêtements). Reportez vous à la page 20. Puis cherchez l'image qui représente une jupe dans la liste et vous trouverez ainsi le mot en anglais.

Pour vérifier l'orthographe d'un mot anglais ...

Pour connaître l'orthographe de *skirt*, regardez à la lettre *s* dans la liste anglais/français ou cherchez le mot en question à la page concernée.

Jeux et activités

Il y a une planche d'activités sur chaque double page qui offre des jeux et activités. Ceux-ci visent à développer les compétences des enfants dans les domaines suivants: classement, reconnaissance du vocabulaire, orthographe, calcul ... . Tous les mots figurant sur ces planches d'activités sont traduits dans la partie bilingue du dictionnaire à la fin de l'ouvrage.

Les jolies illustrations accompagnées de gags visuels faisant référence aux histoires enfantines connues pourront être utilisées de mille façons lors d'activités langagières variées: raconter des histoires, travailler en 'pair work' (travail deux à deux), etc ...

Si vous avez des questions concernant d'autres exploitations possibles de ce dictionnaire, n'hésitez pas à écrire à l'éditeur qui vous fera parvenir une brochure gratuite: Thomas Nelson and Sons Ltd, Nelson House, Mayfield Road, Walton-on-Thames, Surrey, KT12 5PL, UK.

Prononciation

Il existe une cassette d'accompagnement pour ce dictionnaire. Elle offre des enregistrements de tous les mots aussi bien que des chansons et des comptines pour plus de variété et pour un meilleur entraînement à la prononciation.

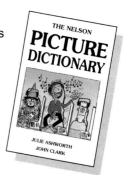

Contents

  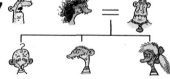 

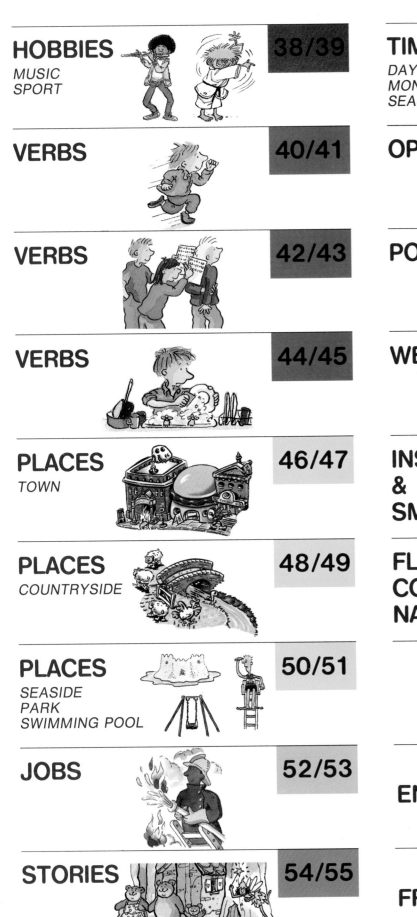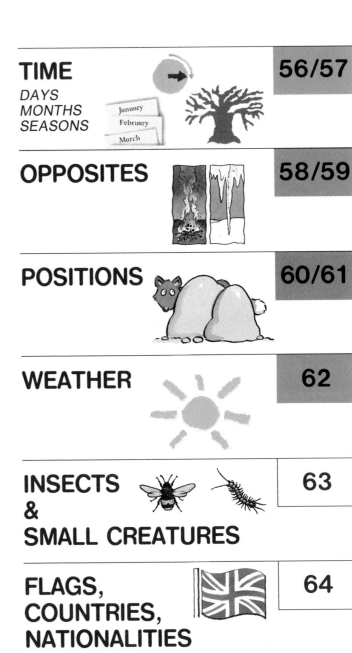

From A to Z

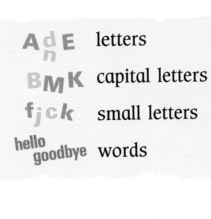

A d n E letters

B M K capital letters

f j c k small letters

hello goodbye words

PUNCTUATION

, comma

• full stop

? question mark

astronaut	jar	queen
balloon	juggler	rainbow
brush	key	rope
cage	kite	snowman
candle	ladder	suitcase
cobweb	letter	telescope
dinosaur	lobster	tortoise
dustbin	magnet	umbrella
envelope	match	vampire
firework	needle	wheel
flag	newspaper	xylophone
grasshopper	octopus	yacht
hammer	pin	yo-yo
igloo	plaster	zip

■ How many letters are there in the alphabet?

■ How many words begin with the letter **l**?

■ How many letters are there in the word **xylophone**?

■ What is the longest word on this page?

■ Write these letters in alphabetical order:

b e i t o n s u y a

■ What are these?

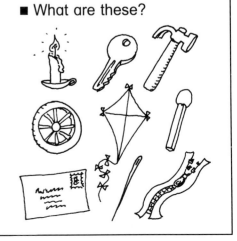

In Space

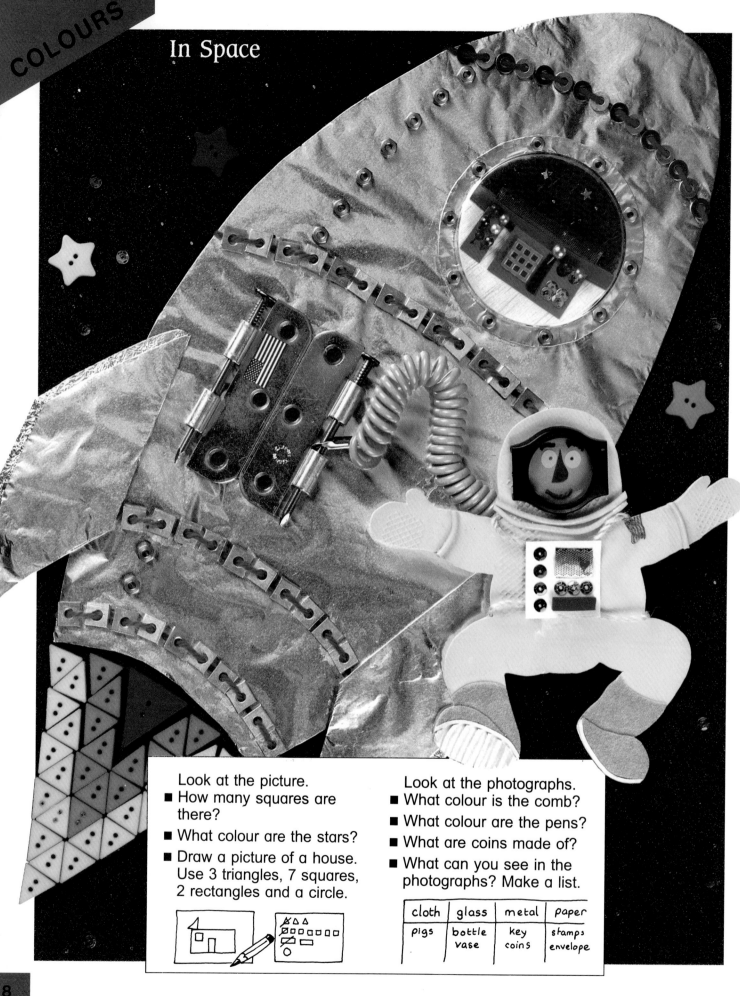

Look at the picture.
- How many squares are there?
- What colour are the stars?
- Draw a picture of a house. Use 3 triangles, 7 squares, 2 rectangles and a circle.

Look at the photographs.
- What colour is the comb?
- What colour are the pens?
- What are coins made of?
- What can you see in the photographs? Make a list.

cloth	glass	metal	paper
pigs	bottle vase	key coins	stamps envelope

COLOURS

MATERIALS

 black

 blue

 brown

 gold

 green

 grey

 orange

 pink

 purple

 red

 silver

 white

 yellow

 cloth

 glass

 metal

 paper

 plastic

 rubber

 wood

wool

SHAPES

 circle

circle | square

 heart

heart | star

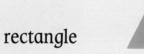 rectangle

rectangle | triangle

0	nought/zero
1	one
2	two
3	three
4	four
5	five
6	six
7	seven
8	eight
9	nine
10	ten
11	eleven
12	twelve
13	thirteen
14	fourteen
15	fifteen
16	sixteen
17	seventeen
18	eighteen
19	nineteen
20	twenty
30	thirty
40	forty
50	fifty
60	sixty
70	seventy
80	eighty
90	ninety
100	a hundred
1,000	a thousand
1,000,000	a million

How many?

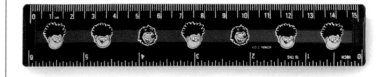

 badge

 ball

 calculator

 car

 clock

 dice

 domino

 playing card

 ruler

FRACTIONS

 half

 quarter

- Find 7 animals in the photograph.
- Find these numbers in the photograph.
  18 57 15 300
- What numbers are on the badges?
- Count from 1 to 10 in English. Then count backwards from 10 to 1.
- How many cars are there?
  How many rulers?
  How many dice?
  Make a chart.

| 1 | clock |
| 2 | calculators |

A Day at School

- Find 9 rats in the picture.
- How many pupils can you see in the language laboratory?
- Write the names of the rooms in alphabetical order.
- What is in your bag? Draw pictures and write the words.

My bag
a pencil case
pencils

ROOMS

1	library	6	science laboratory
2	cloakroom	7	staff room
3	toilet	8	gymnasium/gym
4	hall	9	office
5	language laboratory	10	classroom
		11	playground

bag

crayons

notebook

pen

pencil

pencil case

pencil sharpener

rubber

ruler

TIMETABLE - CLASS 13

	9·00 10·00	10·00 10·30	10·30 11·30	11·30 12·30	12·30 14·00	14·00 15·30
MON	Maths	B R E A K	English	L U N C H	Geography	Physical Education
TUES	Science		History		Music	Art
WED	Geography		Maths		History	English

In the Classroom

bell		file	
bin		glue	
blackboard		light	
board rubber		paintbrush	
bookcase		paper	
box		paperclip	
calculator		plant	
cassette		poster	
chair		pupils	
chalk		scales	
clock		scissors	
compass		shelf	
computer		stapler	
cupboard		sticky tape	
desk		string	
drawer		tape	
drawing		teacher	
drawing pin		video	
easel		whiteboard	

Puppets and Masks

- Find 6 words beginning with the letter **f**.
- Look at the puppets and masks.
  Count the ears. Count the eyes. Count the teeth.
- Which mask has got a long moustache?
- Which mask has got the biggest ears?
- Write these words in alphabetical order:
  beard body back bottom bald
- Draw a puppet or mask with a long nose, big eyes and curly hair. Label your picture.

face

head

tooth (teeth)

tongue

chin

back

elbow

body

bottom

stomach

knee

hair

eyebrow

freckle

leg

ankle

foot (feet)

beard

eyelash

cheek

lip

scar

eye

mouth

neck

shoulder

chest

arm

thumb

finger

hand

forehead

ear

nose

moustache

toe

HAIR

blonde

bald

dark

curly

fair

straight

ginger

The Monster Family

grandfather/
grandad

granddaughter

grandmother/
grandma

granddaughter

father/
dad

daughter

mother/
mum

daughter

brothers

sister

aunts/
aunties

niece

uncles

niece

cousin

cousin

grandparents

grandfather

grandson

grandmother

grandson

parents

father

son

mother

son

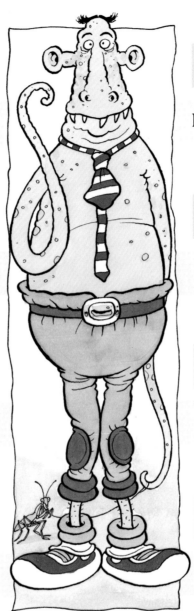

wife

husband

sons

father

daughter

father

nephew

uncle

children

PEOPLE

children

adults

 baby

 boy

 girl

 man

 woman

- How many different monsters are there?
- Rearrange the letters to make words.

ecien	**phenwe**
clune	**ieuatn**
itsesr	**oretbhr**
heomtr	**rehfta**

- The purple monster is called Plum. Give the other monsters a name.
- How many cousins has Plum got? Who is Plum's grandmother? Write some more questions.

- Find 8 different words with 6 letters.
- Make a poster of yourself and your family. Use photos or draw pictures. Label the pictures.

bikini

 boots

 bra

 cardigan

 coat

 dress

 dressing gown

 dungarees

 gloves

 hat

 jacket

 jeans

 jumper/sweater

 knickers

 nightie

 pyjamas

 scarf

 shirt

 shoes

 shorts

 skirt

 slippers

The Campsite

■ Find these things in the picture.
What are they called in English?

■ Work with a friend. Ask some questions about the picture.
e.g. Who's wearing a red dress?
Who's wearing dungarees?

 socks

 sweatshirt

 swimming costume

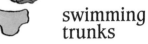 swimming trunks

 tie

 tights

 tracksuit

 trainers

 trousers

 t-shirt

 underpants

 uniform

 vest

JEWELLERY

bracelet

earrings

necklace

ring

belt

button

glasses

hair slide

pocket

ribbon

shoelace

Animals of the World

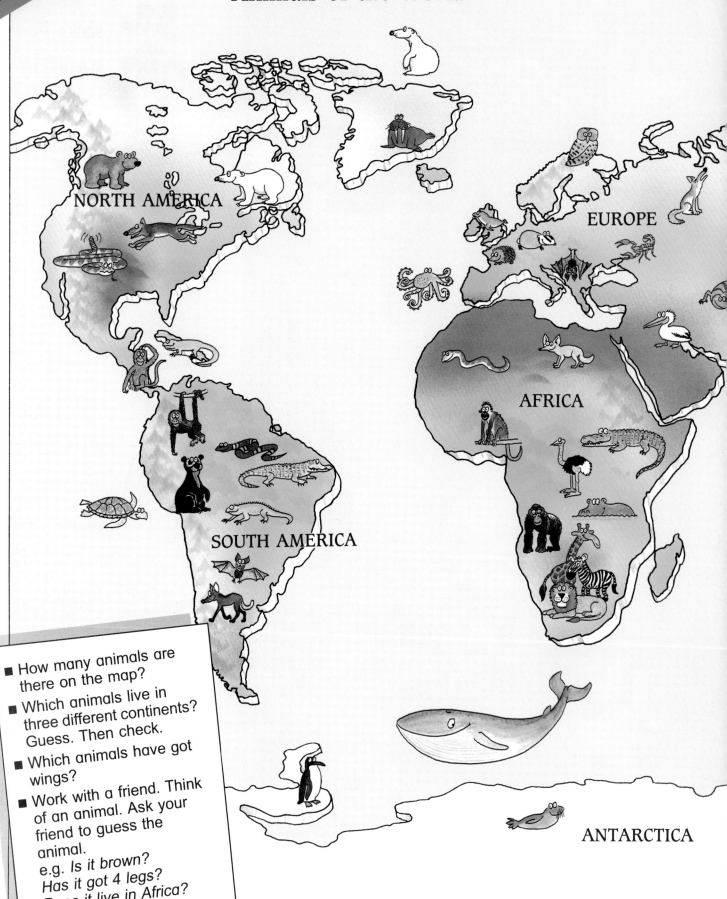

- How many animals are there on the map?
- Which animals live in three different continents? Guess. Then check.
- Which animals have got wings?
- Work with a friend. Think of an animal. Ask your friend to guess the animal.
  e.g. *Is it brown?*
  Has it got 4 legs?
  Does it live in Africa?

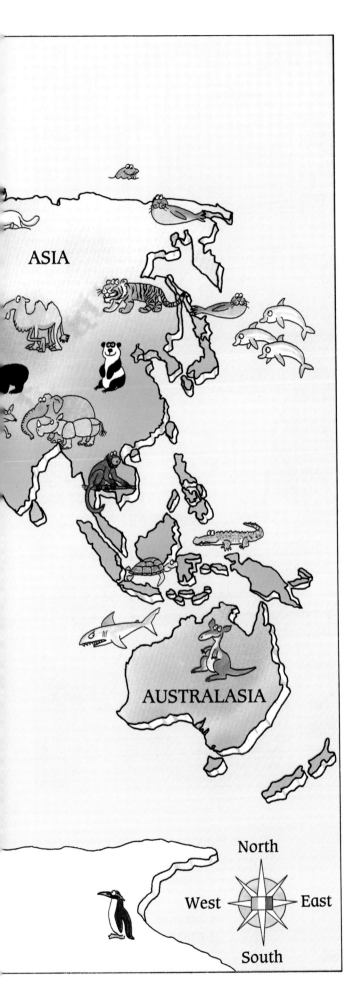

	AFRICA	AMERICA	ANTARCTICA	ASIA	AUSTRALASIA	EUROPE
bat	●	●		●	●	●
bear				●		●
camel	●			●		
crocodile	●	●		●	●	
dolphin	●	●		●	●	●
elephant	●			●		
fox	●	●		●		●
giraffe	●					
gorilla	●					
hedgehog	●			●		●
hippopotamus	●					
kangaroo					●	
lion	●					
lizard	●	●		●	●	●
monkey	●	●		●		
octopus	●	●		●	●	●
ostrich	●					
owl	●	●		●	●	●
panda				●		
pelican	●	●		●	●	●
penguin	●		●		●	
rhinoceros	●			●		
seal	●	●	●		●	●
shark	●	●			●	●
snake	●	●		●	●	●
tiger				●		
turtle	●	●		●	●	●
whale	●	●	●	●	●	●
wolf	●	●		●		●
zebra	●					

Pets

1	budgie	6	frog	11	parrot
2	canary	7	guinea pig	12	puppy
3	cat	8	hamster	13	rabbit
4	dog	9	kitten	14	rat
5	fish	10	mouse	15	tortoise

- How many mice are there in the pet shop?
- Find these things in the pet shop:

  a basket   **a fish tank**
  a cage   **a kennel**

Farm Animals

- How many birds are there on the farm and in the pet shop?
- How many chicks are there on the farm?
- What is a young cow called?
- What colour is the pig?

1	bull	6	donkey	11	horse
2	calf	7	duck	12	lamb
3	chick	8	goat	13	pig
4	cockerel	9	goose	14	piglet
5	cow	10	hen	15	sheep

Fruit and Vegetables

- Find 10 words on this page with 6 letters.
- How many green vegetables are there?
- Work with a friend. Describe a fruit or vegetable.
  e.g. *It's a long orange vegetable.*
  Ask your friend to guess the name.

- Ask your friends:
  Do you like potatoes?
  Do you like apples?
  What's your favourite fruit?
  What's your favourite vegetable?
- Make a list of fruit and vegetables.

fruit	vegetables
apple apricot	asparagus

apple

apricot

beans

cauliflower

celery

cherries

cucumber

grapefruit

grapes

leek

melon

mushroom

onion

orange

papaya

plum

potato

raspberry

spinach

sprouts

asparagus

aubergine

avocado

banana

beetroot

broccoli

cabbage

carrot

coconut

corn

courgette

lemon

lettuce

lime

mango

peach

pear

peas

pepper

pineapple

strawberry

tomato

turnip

watermelon

A Party

birthday cake

biscuit

cheeseburger

chocolate

cola

crisps

doughnut

hamburger

hot dog

- How many candles are there on the birthday cake?
- Find 8 things beginning with the letter **s**.
- Close the dictionary. Can you remember what is on the table?
- What are these?

_ _ _ _ _ _ _   _ _ _ _

_ _ _ _ _   _ _ _ _ _

- What did you eat and drink yesterday? Make a list.

breakfast	lunch	dinner	supper
orange juice cornflakes	salad	chicken rice	toast

DRINKS   ON THE TABLE

 beer

 coffee

 fruit juice

 milk

 tea

 water

 wine

 ketchup

 mustard

 pepper

 salt

 sugar

 vinegar

trifle

sweets

sandwich

pizza

nuts

milkshake

meat

lemonade

jelly

ice cream

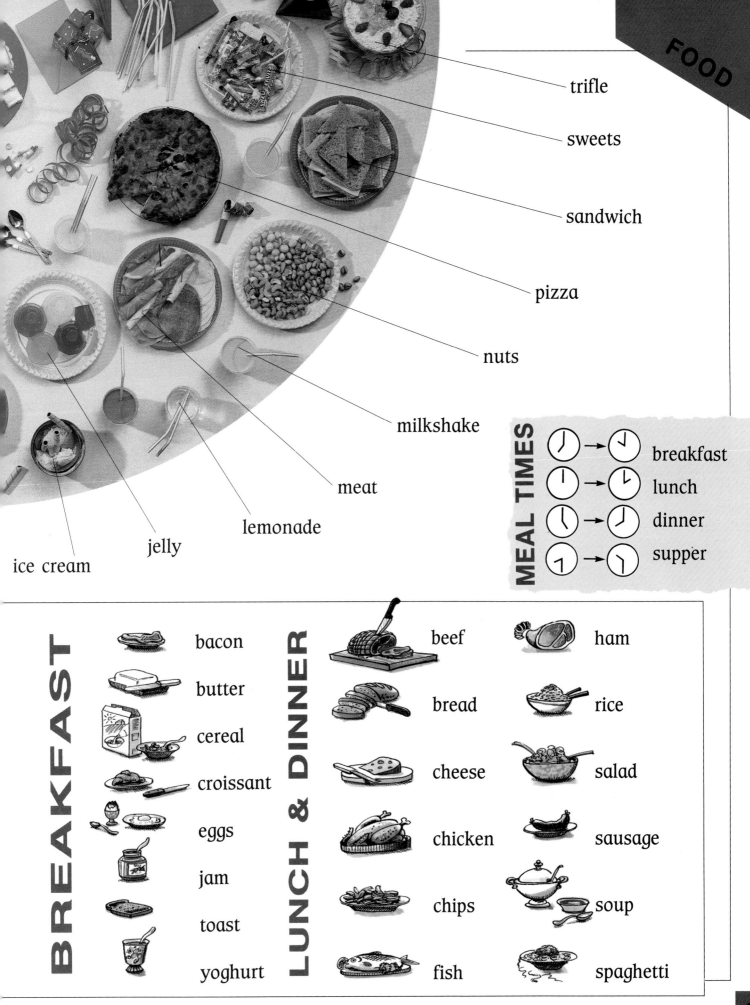

MEAL TIMES

breakfast

lunch

dinner

supper

BREAKFAST

bacon

butter

cereal

croissant

eggs

jam

toast

yoghurt

LUNCH & DINNER

beef

bread

cheese

chicken

chips

fish

ham

rice

salad

sausage

soup

spaghetti

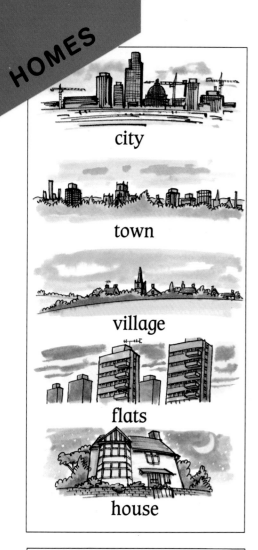

city

town

village

flats

house

Upstairs

bathroom

OUTSIDE

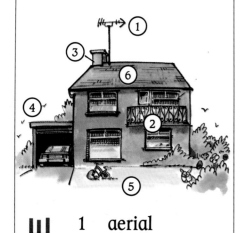

1 aerial
2 balcony
3 chimney
4 garage
5 garden
6 roof

 bath

 bed

 blanket

 carpet

 curtain

 duvet

 lamp

 mirror

 picture

pillow

plug

rug

bedroom

 sheets

 shower

 soap

 tap

 toilet

 toilet paper

 toothbrush

 toothpaste

 towel

 vase

 wardrobe

 washbasin

- Find 10 coins in the picture.
- Find 5 red things in the picture.
- Translate these words:
  bath blanket curtain bed carpet

  Write them in alphabetical order in your language.
- Which things are in the bedroom and which things are in the bathroom? Make a list.

bedroom	bathroom
bed blanket	bath

Downstairs

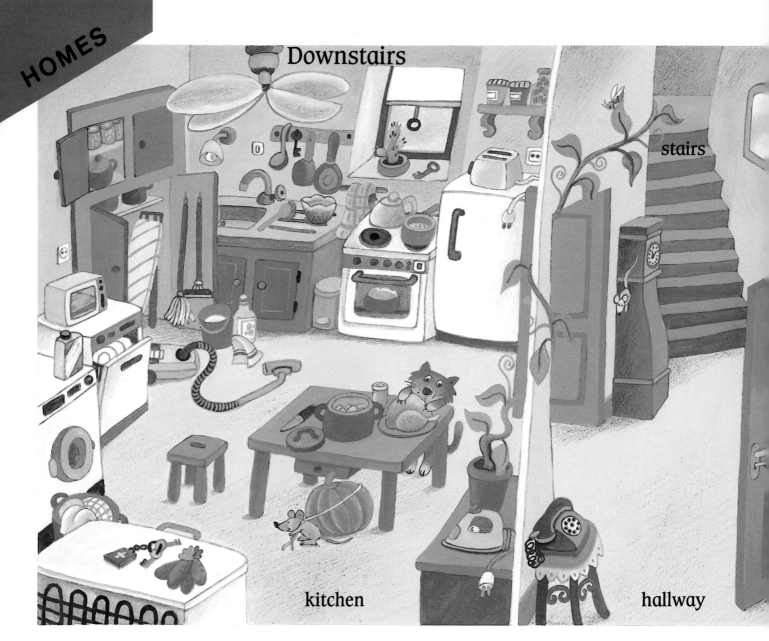

stairs

kitchen

hallway

- Find 10 keys in the picture.
- Find 3 things in the kitchen beginning with the letter **c**.
- Find 3 things in the living room beginning with the letter **p**.
- Close your book. Can you remember what is in the living room?
- What colour is the kettle?
- Write the name of 5 things that are in the living room and in the kitchen too.

 armchair

 blind

 bottle

 cooker

 cushion

 dishwasher

 fan

 freezer

 fridge

 iron

 ironing board

 jar

living/dining room

ON THE TABLE

bowl

cup

fork

glass

knife

mug

plate

saucer

spoon

tablecloth

teapot

 kettle

 microwave

 mop

 oven

 pan

 plug

 sewing machine

 sink

 sofa/settee

 stereo

 stool

 switch

 telephone

 television/TV

 toaster

 tray

 vacuum cleaner

 washing machine

33

Air, Land and Sea

- How many animals are there in the picture?
- Find these things in the picture:
  - **a helmet**
  - **a petrol pump**
  - **a runway**
  - **a satellite**
- Look at the words on page 35. Work with a friend. Ask some questions about spelling. e.g. *How do you spell plane?* Check your friend's answers.

 aeroplane/plane

 airship

 ambulance

 balloon

 barge

 bicycle/bike

 boat

 bus

 canoe

 car

 caravan

 coach

 ferry

 fire engine

 hang glider

 helicopter

 hovercraft

 lorry/truck

 minibus

 motorbike

 parachute

 police car

 pram

 pushchair

 rocket

 roller skates

 scooter

 ship

 skateboard

 space ship

 space shuttle

 speedboat

 submarine

 tank

 train

 tram

 tricycle

 van

 wheelchair

yacht

Ruby's Room

TOYS

 ball

 bat

 bricks

 cards

 clown

 computer game

 doll

 doll's house

 games

 gun

 jigsaw puzzle

 paints

 robot

 skipping rope

 soft toys

 teddy

 train set

 walkie-talkies

PERSONAL THINGS

 books

 camera

 comb

 diary

 football boots

 hairbrush

 hairdryer

 handbag

headphones

 make-up

 money

 money box

 personal stereo

 purse

 sports bag

 torch

 typewriter

 watch

THINGS TO COLLECT

 autographs

 badges

 coins

 comics

 medals

 models

 photographs

 postcards

 stamps

- Find 8 things in the picture beginning with the letter **c**.
- Which of these things is not in the picture?

  a car
  a doll
  a medal
  a purse
  a robot
  a watch

- Connect the words.

computer	**rope**
skipping	**puzzle**
money	**dryer**
photo	**game**
jigsaw	**boots**
hair	**album**
football	**box**

- Work with a friend. Ask some questions about the picture.
  e.g. Where's the purse?
  What colour's the comb?

Music

INSTRUMENTS

1	banjo	8	guitar	15	synthesizer
2	cello	9	harp	16	tambourine
3	clarinet	10	maracas	17	triangle
4	cymbals	11	mouth organ	18	trombone
5	double bass	12	piano	19	trumpet
6	drums	13	recorder	20	violin
7	flute	14	saxophone	21	xylophone

- Which instruments do you blow?
- Cover the words on page 38. Can you remember the names of the instruments? Check your answers and try again.
- What is the difference between a double bass and a cello?

Sport

athletics

baseball

basketball

cricket

football

golf

gymnastics

horse riding

ice skating

judo

skiing

swimming

■ In which sports do you use these things?

■ Rearrange the letters and make words.

ktreicc   **llabbtaeks**
nnstie   **lfloaobt**

table tennis

tennis

The Action Board Game

This is a board game for two or more players.

You need:

 dice

counters

Rules

1. Put your counters on START.

2. Throw the dice. Move your counter.

3. When you land on a square, do the action, e.g. cough if you land on square 4.

4. If you do the action wrongly, miss a turn.

5. The first player to reach FINISH is the winner.

- Find these things in the pictures:

  a bottle   **a pencil**
  a lamp   **a stool**

- Say this rhyme and do the actions.

  Point to the ceiling,
  Touch the floor.
  Open the window,
  And close the door.

- What are the boys and girls doing? Make a list.

boys	girls
close	blow
	clap

START

1 blow

2 clap

15 laugh

14 kneel

13 GO BACK 4 SQUARES

16 open

17 pick up

18 point

31 touch

30 GO FORWARD 6 SQUARES

29 stand up

32 turn off

33 turn on

34 walk

close

cough

crawl

cry

dance

jump

hop

fall

drop

draw

read

run

MISS A TURN

scratch

scream

smile

sit down

sing

shout

shake

wave

whisper

whistle

write

FINISH

In the Playground

1	argue	13	fight	25	measure
2	bite	14	fish	26	paint
3	bounce	15	fly	27	pull
4	build	16	give	28	push
5	buy	17	hide	29	ride
6	carry	18	hit	30	skate
7	catch	19	hug	31	ski
8	climb	20	juggle	32	skip
9	copy	21	kick	33	swim
10	dig	22	kiss	34	take
11	dive	23	knock	35	tear
12	drive	24	lift	36	throw

■ How many children are there in the playground?
How many boys? How many girls?

■ What are they doing?

He's throwing a ball.   *She's juggling.*   *They're arguing.*

Point to the children in the picture. Ask your friend:
What's he doing?
What's she doing?

■ Pick a number from 1 to 36. Say the number.
Ask your friend to mime the action.

■ There are five letters in the picture.
Find the letters and make a word.

■ Ask your friends:
Can you swim?   *Can you skate?*
Can you ski?   *Can you juggle?*
Draw a graph.

In the Home

break

brush

clean

dream

drink

dry

go to bed

have a bath

have a shower

mend

peel

pour

stretch

sweep

take off

wash

wash up

watch

comb

cook

cut

eat

get dressed

get up

iron

knit

listen

put on

sew

sleep

tie

wake up

weigh

yawn

- Find these things in the pictures:

  an apple   **an iron**
  a cake   **a towel**

- All of these words are verbs. Which words are also nouns?

  **comb drink eat iron
  listen**

- Mime one of the actions. Ask a friend to guess what you are doing.
  e.g. *Are you washing your hands?*

The Town

How many animals are there in the picture?

Find these things in the picture:
a bottle
a guitar
a pan
a spaceship

BUILDINGS

1	airport	7	factory
2	bank	8	hospital
3	cafe	9	hotel
4	car park	10	market
5	church	11	mosque
6	cinema	12	museum

46

Work with a friend. Imagine you are hiding in the town. Ask your friend to guess where you are hiding.

e.g. *Are you in a building?*

Translate the names of the buildings. Which words are the same in your language?

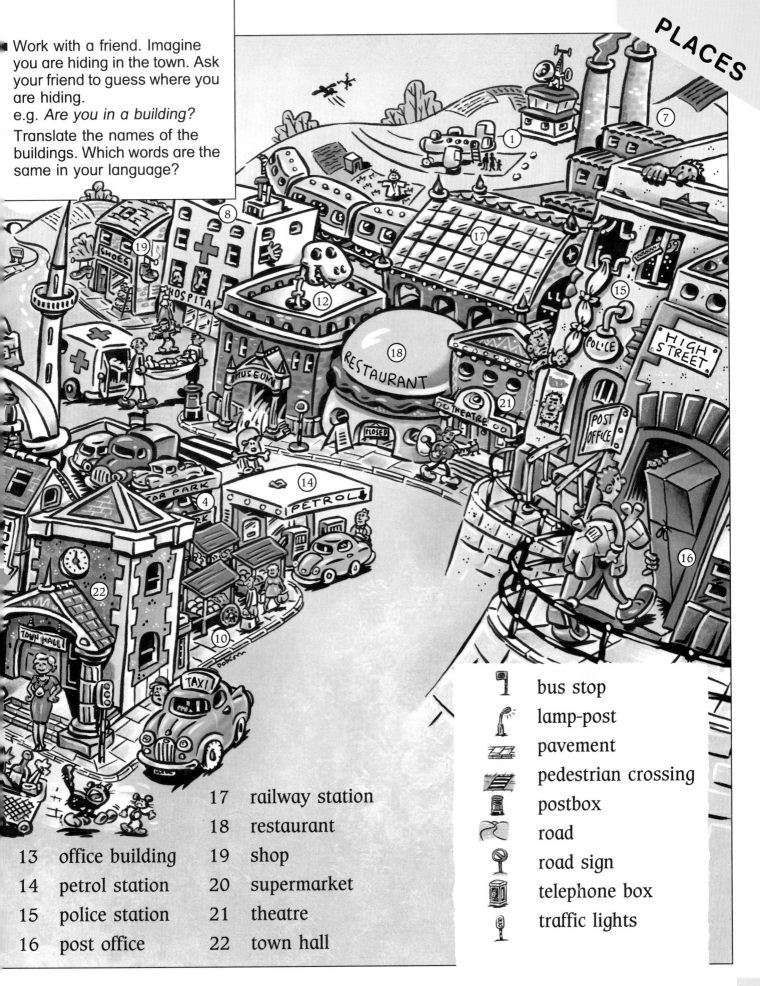

	bus stop
	lamp-post
	pavement
	pedestrian crossing
	postbox
	road
	road sign
	telephone box
	traffic lights

13	office building
14	petrol station
15	police station
16	post office
17	railway station
18	restaurant
19	shop
20	supermarket
21	theatre
22	town hall

The Countryside

- How many different animals are there in the picture?
- Find 8 things beginning with the letter **s**.
- Find these things in the picture:
    - **a fire**
    - **a hammock**
    - **a nest**
    - **a scarecrow**
    - **a stone**
- What is the difference between a mountain and a hill?

barn

bush

farmhouse

fence

fire

gate

hammock

haystack

leaves

litter

nest

picnic

pylon

rucksack

scarecrow

signpost

smoke

stick

stone

tent

tractor

tree

1	bridge	7	hill	13	river
2	canal	8	lake	14	rubbish tip
3	cave	9	motorway	15	stream
4	field	10	mountain	16	tunnel
5	forest	11	power station	17	valley
6	grass	12	reservoir	18	waterfall

The Seaside

sky

cliff

sea

beach

bucket	
crab	
deckchair	
feather	
island	
lighthouse	
pebbles	
rocks	
sand	

sand castle	
seaweed	
shells	
spade	
starfish	
sunglasses	
suntan lotion	
surfboard	
waves	

- ■ Find these things in the pictures:

  flowers   **a slide**
  goggles   **a swing**

- ■ Find two things that are in all three pictures.

- ■ Find a picture of the seaside or a swimming pool in a magazine. Stick the picture on a sheet of paper. Label the picture.

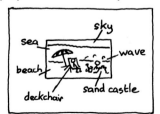

The Park

The Swimming Pool

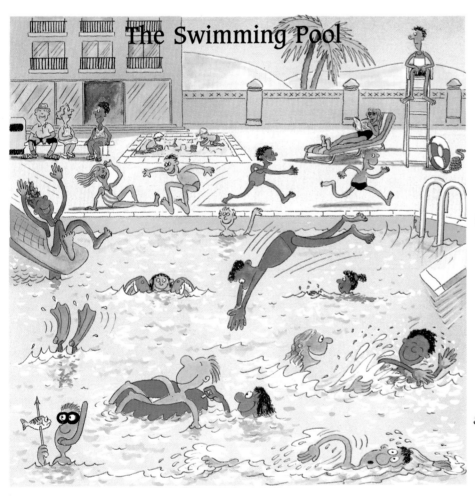

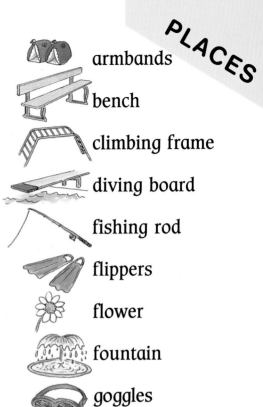 armbands

bench

climbing frame

diving board

fishing rod

flippers

flower

fountain

goggles

lifeguard

litter bin

pond

rope

 roundabout

rubber ring

sandpit

seesaw

slide

snorkel

swing

water

wheelbarrow

When I grow up...

1 actor 2 actress 3 artist 4 bank clerk 5 builder

10 doctor 11 electrician 12 fireman

15 nurse 16 pilot 17 plumber

■ What are these things called in English? Who uses them?

21 secretary 22 shop assistant 23 singer

6   bus driver

7   chef

8   dancer

9   dentist

13   hairdresser

14   mechanic

18   policewoman

19   postman

20   scientist

Rearrange the letters to make words.

irbleud   crsaeyetr
etv   mlbrpue

Work with a friend.
Point to a boy or a girl in the picture. Ask your friend:
What does he want to be?
What does she want to be?

What do you want to be?
Ask your friends.

24   vet

25   waiter

26   waitress

Once upon a time...

- Find 4 things beginning with the letter **c**.
- How many **crowns** are there in the picture?
- Are these sentences true or false?
  The giant is holding an axe.
  The skeleton is flying on the broomstick.
  The dragon is red.
  The pirate is wearing a crown.

STORYBOOK CHARACTERS

1 alien
2 dragon
3 fairy
4 genie
5 ghost
6 giant
7 king
8 mermaid
9 monster
10 pirate
11 prince
12 princess
13 queen
14 skeleton
15 vampire
16 witch
17 wizard

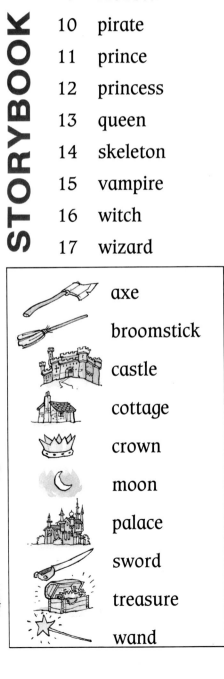

axe
broomstick
castle
cottage
crown
moon
palace
sword
treasure
wand

The Calendar

Monday	**1** first	**8** eighth	**15** fifteenth	**22** twenty-second	**29** twenty-ninth
Tuesday	**2** second	**9** ninth	**16** sixteenth	**23** twenty-third	**30** thirtieth
Wednesday	**3** third	**10** tenth	**17** seventeenth	**24** twenty-fourth	**31** thirty-first
Thursday	**4** fourth	**11** eleventh	**18** eighteenth	**25** twenty-fifth	
Friday	**5** fifth	**12** twelfth	**19** nineteenth	**26** twenty-sixth	
Saturday	**6** sixth	**13** thirteenth	**20** twentieth	**27** twenty-seventh	
Sunday	**7** seventh	**14** fourteenth	**21** twenty-first	**28** twenty-eighth	

weekend

1st first   **2**nd second   **3**rd third   **4**th fourth

MONTHS

January
February
March
April
May
June
July
August
September
October
November
December

Mon	1	8	15	22	29
Tue	2	9	16	23	30
Wed	3	10	17	24	31
Thur	4	11	18	25	
Fri	5	12	19	26	
Sat	6	13	20	27	
Sun	7	14	21	28	

WHAT'S THE TIME?

quarter to...

quarter past...

half past...

...o'clock

a.m.

midday

p.m.

midnight

60 seconds = 1 minute
60 minutes = 1 hour
24 hours = 1 day
7 days = 1 week
52 weeks = 1 year

 morning
06.00 – 12.00

 afternoon
12.00 – 18.00

evening
18.00 – 24.00

night
24.00 – 06.00

■ What's the time?

■ Write the days of the week in alphabetical order.

■ Say the months in English backwards.

■ What is the date today?

■ What was the date yesterday?

■ When is your birthday? Ask your friends. Draw a graph.

January	▨			
February	▨▨			
March	▨			

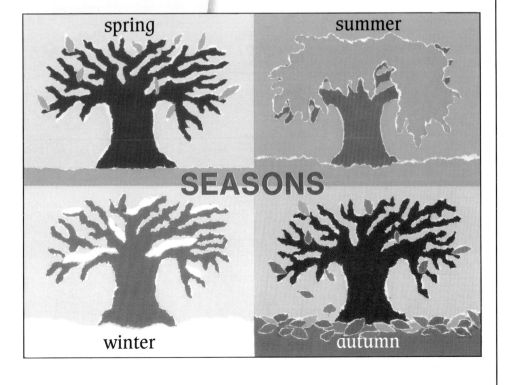

spring

summer

SEASONS

winter

autumn

57

Beautiful or ugly?

- Find 5 words beginning with the letter **c**.
- Say a word. Ask your friend to say the opposite.
- Which words mean the same?

closed	big
difficult	dear
expensive	hard
large	little
loud	noisy
small	shut

- Which words describe each picture?

cold   long
fat   sharp
light

beautiful / ugly

big/large / little/small

day / night

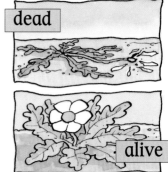
dead / alive

front / back

good / bad

happy / sad

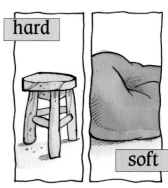
hard / soft

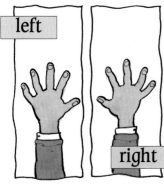
left / right

long / short

new / old

noisy/loud / quiet

rough / smooth

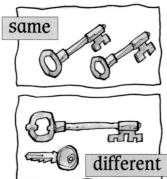
same / different

short / tall

strong / weak

blunt — sharp

cheap — expensive/dear

clean — dirty

dark — light

easy — difficult/hard

empty — full

fast — slow

fat — thin

heavy — light

here — there

high — low

hot — cold

old — young

open — closed/shut

rich — poor

right — wrong

stupid — clever

thick — thin

top — bottom

wet — dry

Where is it?

above

The rat is **above** the hat.

duck   hen

The birds are **above** the words.

behind

The fox is **behind** the rocks.

The frog is sitting **behind** the dog.

between

The fox is **between** the rocks.

down

The bears are walking **down** the stairs.

in

There is a mouse **in** the house.

The fish is **in** the dish.

in front of

The fox is **in front of** the rocks.

The frog is sitting **in front of** the dog.

into

The slug is crawling **into** the jug.

near

The cat is **near** the rat.

Where are the frogs?

next to/by

The rat is **next to** the hat.

on

The cat is **on** the mat.

There are two pictures **on** the wall, one is big and one is small.

out of

There's a witch on a broom flying **out of** the room.

over

There's a snake crawling **over** the cake.

under

There is a hare **under** the chair.

duck   hen

The words are **under** the birds.

up

The bears are walking **up** the stairs.

- Find 3 things beginning with the letter **f.**
- What are these?

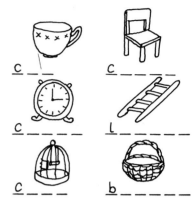

c _ _   c _ _ _ _

c _ _ _ _   l _ _ _ _ _

c _ _ _   b _ _ _ _ _

- Work with a friend. Ask some questions about the frogs.
  e.g. *Where's the green frog?*
  Where's the blue frog?
  Is the red frog under the chair?

- **Fish** rhymes with **dish.** Connect the words that rhyme.

birds	hair
chair	box
frog	words
rat	dog
rocks	hat

- Find 8 words in the puzzle.

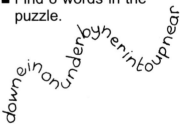

downeinonunderbyherintoupnear

What's the weather like?

It's cloudy. It's warm.

It's foggy.

It's raining. It's wet.

It's snowing. It's cold.

It's sunny. It's hot.

It's windy.

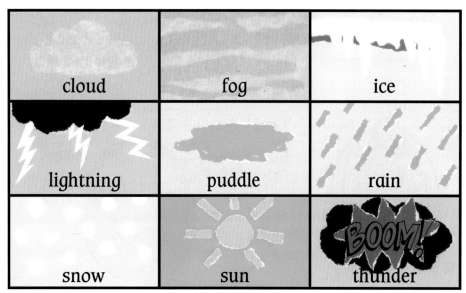

cloud

fog

ice

lightning

puddle

rain

snow

sun

thunder

- Find these things in the pictures:
  a bucket
  a kite
  a glove
  sunglasses
- Copy the puzzle. Write the words.

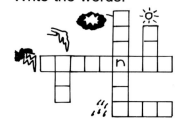

Insects and small creatures

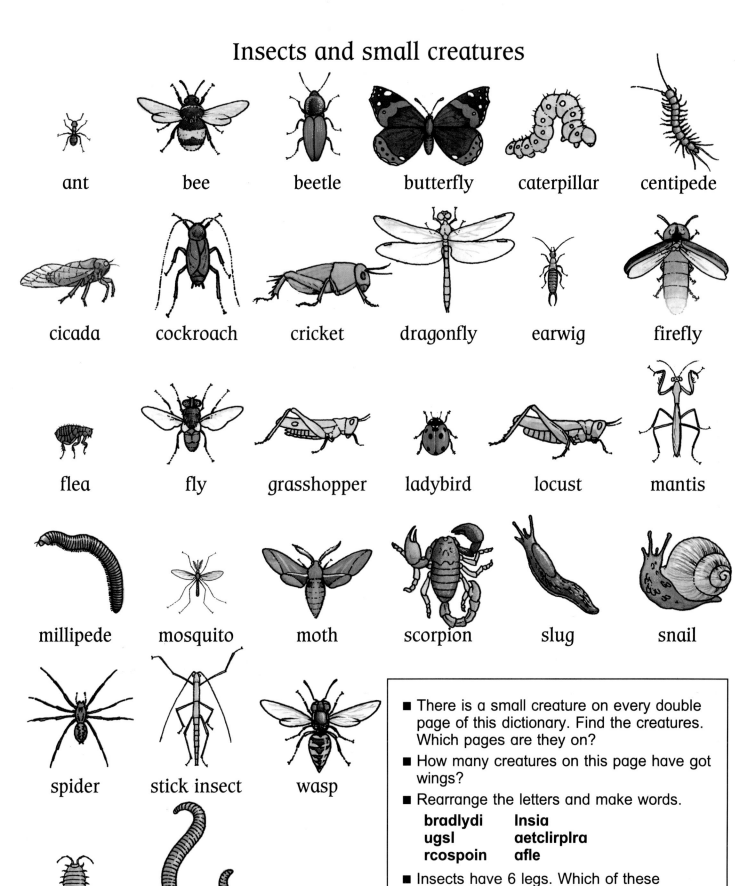

ant   bee   beetle   butterfly   caterpillar   centipede

cicada   cockroach   cricket   dragonfly   earwig   firefly

flea   fly   grasshopper   ladybird   locust   mantis

millipede   mosquito   moth   scorpion   slug   snail

spider   stick insect   wasp

woodlouse   worm

- There is a small creature on every double page of this dictionary. Find the creatures. Which pages are they on?
- How many creatures on this page have got wings?
- Rearrange the letters and make words.

  bradlydi   **lnsia**
  ugsl   **aetclirplra**
  rcospoin   **afle**

- Insects have 6 legs. Which of these creatures are not insects?

  ant   **fly**   **millipede**   **snail**
  beetle   **mantis**   **slug**   **spider**

Flags, Countries and Nationalities

Argentina
Argentinian

Australia
Australian

Austria
Austrian

Belgium
Belgian

Brazil
Brazilian

Canada
Canadian

Chile
Chilean

Denmark
Danish

Eire
Irish

Finland
Finnish

France
French

Germany
German

Greece
Greek

India
Indian

Italy
Italian

Japan
Japanese

Mexico
Mexican

The Netherlands
Dutch

New Zealand
New Zealander

Norway
Norwegian

Peru
Peruvian

Portugal
Portuguese

Spain
Spanish

Sweden
Swedish

Switzerland
Swiss

Turkey
Turkish

The U.K.
British

The U.S.A.
American

Venezuela
Venezuelan

- There is a flag on every double page of this dictionary. Find the flags. Which pages are they on?
- How many flags are red, white and blue?
- Which flag is blue and yellow?
- How many stars are there on the American flag?
- Which flags are these?

AaBbCcDdEeFfGgHhIiJjKkLlMm

Wordlists

Les pages 66 – 81 proposent une liste alphabétique en anglais de tous les mots du dictionnaire. Chaque mot est accompagné de se traduction en français suivi du numéro de la page qui mentionne le mot concerné. (Cette liste comporte également tous les mots figurant sur les planches d'activités.)

Les pages 82 – 96 proposent une liste alphabétique en français de tous les mots du dictionnaire. Chaque mot est accompagné de sa traduction en anglais suivi du numéro de la page qui mentionne le mot concerné.

NnOoPpQqRrSsTtUuVvWwXxYyZz

English–French

a

a un, une 12
above au-dessus de 60
about sur 20
action action 40
actor acteur 52
actress actrice 52
adult adulte 19
aerial antenne 30
aeroplane avion 35
Africa Afrique 23
afternoon après-midi 57
again encore, de nouveau 38
air air 34
airport aéroport 46
airship dirigeable 35
album album 36
alien extra-terrestre 55
alive vivant 58
all tout, toute, tous, toutes 45
ALPHABET alphabet 6-7
alphabetical alphabétique 7
also aussi 45
ambulance ambulance 35
America Amérique 23
American américain 64
and et 8
ANIMALS animaux 22-25
ankle cheville 16
answer réponse 34
ant fourmi 63
Antarctica l'Antarctique 23
apple pomme 26
apricot abricot 26
April avril 57
are (be) sont (être) 60
Argentina Argentine 64
Argentinian argentin 64
argue se disputer 43
arm bras 17
armband bouée pour les bras 51
armchair fauteuil 32
art dessin 13

artist artiste 52
Asia Asie 23
ask poser (une question) 20; demander à 22
asparagus asperges 27
astronaut astronaute 7
at à 12
athletics athlétisme 39
aubergine aubergine 27
August août 57
aunt tante 18; aunties tantes 18
Australasia Australasie 23
Australia Australie 64
Australian australien 64
Austria Autriche 64
Austrian autrichien 64
autograph autographe 37
autumn automne 57
avocado avocat (poire) 27
axe hache 55

b

baby bébé 19
back dos 16; arriere 58; de retour, en retour 41
backwards à l'envers, à rebours 11
bacon lard 29
bad mauvais, méchant 58
badge badge 11, 37
bag sac 13
balcony balcon 30
bald chauve 17
ball boule 11; balle 37
balloon ballon 7; montgolfière 35
banana banane 27
banjo banjo 38
bank banque 46
bank clerk employé(e) de banque 52
barge chaland, péniche 35
barn grange 49
baseball base-ball 39
basket corbeille 24
basketball basket-ball 39
bat chauve-souris 23; batte 37
bath baignoire 30
bathroom salle de bains 30
be être 52–53

beach plage 50
bean haricot 26
bear ours 23
beard barbe 16
beautiful beau, belle 58
bed lit 30
bedroom chambre (à coucher) 31
bee abeille 63
beef bœuf (*viande*) 29
beer bière 28
beetle scarabée 63
beetroot betterave 27
begin commencer 7
behind derrière 60
Belgian belge 64
Belgium Belgique 64
bell sonnerie 15
belt ceinture 21
bench banc 51
between entre 60
bicycle bicyclette 35
big grand, gros 58
biggest (le) plus grand 16
bike vélo 35
bikini bikini 20
bin corbeille à papier 15
bird oiseau 60
birthday anniversaire 57; birthday cake gâteau d'anniversaire 28
biscuit (petit) gâteau sec, biscuit 28
bite mordre 43
black noir 9
blackboard tableau noir 15
blanket couverture (*de lit*) 30
blind store 32
blonde blond 17
blow souffler (*dans*) 38; souffler 40
blue bleu 9
blunt épointé, mal taillé 59
board game jeu de société (*qui se joue sur un tapis*) 40
board rubber brosse à tableau 15
boat bateau 35
BODY corps 16-17
book livre 37
bookcase bibliothèque (*meuble*) 15
boot botte 20
bottle bouteille 32
bottom derrière 16; bas 59

bounce rebondir, faire rebondir 43
bowl bol 33
box boîte 15
boy garçon 19
bra soutien-gorge 20
bracelet bracelet 21
Brazil Brésil 64
Brazilian brésilien 64
bread pain 29
break récréation 13; casser 44
breakfast petit déjeuner 29
brick cube 37
bridge pont 49
British britannique 64
broccoli brocoli 27
broom balai 61
broomstick manche à balai 55
brother frère 18
brown brun 9
brush brosse, (*broom*) balai 7; (se) laver (les dents) 44
bucket seau 50
budgie perruche 24
build bâtir 43
builder maçon 52
building bâtiment 46
bull taureau 25
bus autobus 35
bus driver conducteur d'autobus 53
bush buisson 49
bus stop arrêt d'autobus 47
butter beurre 29
butterfly papillon 63
button bouton 21
buy acheter 43
by à côté de 61

C

cabbage chou 27
cafe café, café-restaurant 46
cage cage 7
cake gâteau 45
calculator calculatrice 11,15
calendar calendrier 56
calf veau (*animal*) 25

call   appeler 19
camel   chameau 23
camera   appareil-photo 37
campsite   camping (*terrain de*) 20
can   pouvoir 8
Canada   Canada 64
Canadian   canadien 64
canal   canal 49
canary   serin 24
candle   bougie 7
canoe   canoë 35
capital   majuscule 7
car   voiture 11, 35
caravan   caravane 35
card   carte 37
cardigan   gilet (de laine) 20
car park   parking 46
carpet   tapis 30
carrot   carotte 27
carry   porter (*dans les bras*) 43
cassette   cassette 15
castle   château (fort) 55
cat   chat 24
catch   attraper 43
caterpillar   chenille 63
cauliflower   chou-fleur 26
cave   caverne 49
ceiling   plafond 14
celery   céleri 26
cello   violoncelle 38
centipede   mille-pattes 63
cereal   céréale 29
chair   chaise 15
chalk   craie 15
character   personnage 55
chart   tableau 11
cheap   bon marché 59
check   vérifier 22
cheek   joue 17
cheese   fromage 29
cheeseburger   hamburger au fromage 28
chef   chef de cuisine 53
cherries   cerises 26
cherry   cerise 26
chest   poitrine 17
chick   poussin 25
chicken   poulet 29
child   enfant 19
children   enfants 19

Chile   Chili 64
Chilean   chilien 64
chimney   cheminée 30
chin   menton 16
chip   frite 29
chocolate   chocolat 28
church   église 46
cicada   cigale, (gros) cri-cri 63
cinema   cinéma 46
circle   cercle 9
circus   cirque 36
city   (grande) ville 30
clap   battre les mains 40
clarinet   clarinette 38
class   classe 13
classroom   salle de classe 12
clean   nettoyer 44; propre 59
clever   intelligent 59
cliff   falaise 50
climb   grimper sur 43
climbing frame   cage à poules, cage à écureuil 51
cloakroom   vestiaire 12
clock   pendule 11; horloge 15
close   fermer 41
closed   fermé 47, 59
cloth   tissu 9
CLOTHES   vêtements 20-21
cloud   nuage 62
cloudy   nuageux 62
clown   clown 37
coach   car 35
coat   manteau 20
cobweb   (vieille) toile d'araignée 7
cockerel   coq 25
cockroach   cafard 63
coconut   noix de coco 27
coffee   café 28
coin   pièce de monnaie 37
cola   coca ® 28
cold   froid 59, 62
collect   collectionner 37
COLOURS   couleurs 8-9
comb   peigne 37; peigner 45
comic   magazine de bandes dessinées 37
comma   virgule 7
compass   compas 15
computer   ordinateur 15
computer game   jeu électronique 37

connect   relier, joindre 37
continent   continent 22
cook   faire la cuisine, faire cuire 45
cooker   cuisinière (*appareil*) 32
copy   copier 43
corn   maïs 27
cottage   petite maison (*à la campagne*) 55
cough   tousser 41
count   compter 11
counter   jeton 40
country   pays 64
countryside   campagne 48
courgette   courgette 27
cousin   cousin 18
cover   couvrir 38
cow   vache 25
crab   crabe 50
crawl   marcher à quatre pattes 41
crayon   crayon de couleur 13
creature   créature, bestiole 63
cricket   cricket 39; grillon, cri-cri 63
crisp   chip 28
crocodile   crocodile 23
croissant   croissant 29
crown   couronne 55
cry   pleurer 41
cucumber   concombre 27
cup   tasse 33
cupboard   placard 15
curly   frisé, bouclé 17
curtain   rideau 30
cushion   coussin 32
cut   couper 45
cymbal   cymbale 38

d

dad   papa 18
dance   danser 41
dancer   danseur, danseuse 53
Danish   danois 64
dark   foncé, brun 17; obscur 59
date   date 57
daughter   fille (*d'une mère, d'un père*) 18
day   jour, journée 57, 58
dead   mort 58

dear   cher 59
December   décembre 57
deckchair   transat 50
Denmark   Danemark 64
dentist   dentiste 53
describe   décrire 26
desk   bureau, pupitre 15
diary   agenda 37
dice   dé 11
dictionary   dictionnaire 28
difference   différence 38
different   différent 58
difficult   difficile 59
dig   creuser 43
dining room   salle à manger 33
dinner   dîner 29
dinosaur   dinosaure 7
dirty   sale 59
dish   plat 60
dishwasher   lave-vaisselle 32
dive   plonger 43
diving board   plongeoir 51
do   faire 40
doctor   docteur 52
dog   chien 24
doll   poupée 37
doll's house   maison de poupée 37
dolphin   dauphin 23
domino   domino 11
donkey   âne 25
door   porte 15
double   double 63
double bass   contrebasse 38
doughnut   beignet 28
down   en bas, vers le bas 60
downstairs   en bas, au rez-de-chaussée 32
dragon   dragon 55
dragonfly   libellule 63
draw   dessiner 41
drawer   tiroir 15
drawing   dessin 15
drawing pin   punaise (*à papier*) 15
dream   rêver 44
dress   robe 20
dressing gown   robe de chambre 20
drink   boisson 28; boire 44
drive   conduire 43
drop   laisser tomber 41
drum   tambour 38

dry sécher, essuyer 44; sec, sèche 59
duck canard 25
dungarees salopette 20
dustbin poubelle, boîte à ordures 7
Dutch hollandais 64
duvet couette 30

each chaque 14
ear oreille 17
earring boucle d'oreille 21
earwig perce-oreille 63
easel chevalet 15
east est 23
easy facile 59
eat manger 45
e.g. par exemple 40
egg œuf 29
eight huit 10
eighteen dix-huit 10
eighty quatre-vingts 10
Eire la République d'Irlande 64
elbow coude 16
electrician électricien 52
elephant éléphant 23
eleven onze 10
empty vide 59
English anglais 13
entrance entrée 12
envelope enveloppe 7
Europe Europe 23
evening soir, soirée 57
every chaque, tout 63
exit sortie 46
expensive cher, coûteux 59
eye œil 17
eyebrow sourcil 16
eyelash cil 17

face visage 16

factory usine 46
fair blond 17
fairy fée 55
fall tomber 41
false faux, fausse 54
FAMILY famille 18-19
fan ventilateur 32
farm ferme 25
farmhouse ferme 49
fast rapide, vite 59
fat gros, gras 59
father père 18
favourite favori, favourite, préféré 26
feather plume 50
February février 57
feet pieds 16
fence clôture 49
ferry ferry 35
field champ 49
fifteen quinze 10
fifty cinquante 10
fight se battre 43
file classeur 15
film film 46
find trouver 11
finger doigt 17
finish arrivée 41
Finland Finlande 64
Finnish finlandais 64
fire feu 49
fire engine voiture de pompiers 35
firefly luciole 63
fireman pompier 52
firework fusée de feu d'artifice 7
first premier 56
fish poisson 24, 29; pêcher 43
fish tank aquarium 24
fishing rod canne à pêche 51
five cinq 10
flag drapeau 7, 64
flat appartement 30; flats immeuble (*de résidence*) 30
flea puce 63
flipper palme 51
floor plancher 15
flower fleur 51
flute flûte 38
fly mouche 63; voler 43
fog brouillard 62

foggy   brumeux 62
FOOD   nourriture 26-29
foot   pied 16
football   football 39
football boot   chaussure de football 37
for   pour 40
forehead   front 17
forest   forêt 49
fork   fourchette 33
forty   quarante 10
forward   en avant 40
fountain   fontaine 51
four   quatre 10
fourteen   quatorze 10
fourth   quatrième 56
fox   renard 23
fraction   fraction 11
France   France 64
freckle   tache de rousseur 16
freezer   congélateur 32
French   français 64
Friday   vendredi 56
fridge   frigo 32
friend   ami, amie 14
frog   grenouille 24
from   de 6
front   avant 58; in front of   devant 60
fruit   fruit, fruits 26; fruit juice   jus de fruit 28
full   plein 59
full stop   point 7

g

game   jeu 37
garage   garage 30
garden   jardin 30
gate   porte 49
genie   djinn 55
geography   géographie 13
German   allemand 64
Germany   Allemagne 64
get dressed   s'habiller 45
get up   se lever (le matin) 45
ghost   fantôme 55
giant   géant 55
ginger   roux, rousse 17

giraffe   girafe 23
girl   fille, jeune fille, fillette 19
give   donner 43
glass   verre 9, 33
glasses   lunettes 21
glove   gant 20
glue   colle 15
go   aller 40, 44
goat   chèvre 25
goggles   lunettes de plongée 51
gold   or, couleur or 9
golf   golf 39
good   bon, sage 58
goose   oie 25
gorilla   gorille 23
grandad   grand-père 18
granddaughter   petit-fille 18
grandfather   grand-père 18
grandmother   grand-mère 18
grandparents   grands-parents 18
grandson   petit-fils 19
grape   raisin 26
grapefruit   pamplemousse 26
graph   graphique 43
grass   herbe 49
grasshopper   sauterelle 7, 63
Greece   Grèce 64
Greek   grec, grecque 64
green   vert 9
grey   gris 9
grow up   devenir adulte 52
guess   deviner 14
guinea pig   cochon d'Inde 24
guitar   guitare 38
gun   pistolet 37
gym   gymnase 12
gymnasium   gymnase 12
gymnastics   gymnastique 39

h

hair   cheveux 16
hairbrush   brosse à cheveux 37
hairdresser   coiffeur, coiffeuse 53
hairdryer   sèche-cheveux 37
hair slide   barrette 21

half   demi 11
half past   et demie 57
hall   (grande) salle 12
hallway   hall d'entrée 32
ham   jambon 29
hamburger   hamburger 28
hammer   marteau 7
hammock   hamac 49
hamster   hamster 24
hand   main 17
handbag   sac à main 37
hang glider   deltaplane 35
happy   heureux 58
hard   dur 58; dur, difficile 59
hare   lièvre 61
harp   harpe 38
has; has got   a 16
hat   chapeau 20
have   avoir, prendre (*une douche, etc*) 44
haystack   meule de foin 49
he   il 43
head   tête 16
headphones   (casque à) écouteurs 37
heart   cœur 9
heavy   lourd 59
hedgehog   hérisson 23
helicopter   hélicoptère 35
helmet   casque 34
hen   poule 25
here   ici 59
hide   cacher, se cacher 43
high   haut 59
hill   colline 49
hippopotamus   hippopotame 23
history   histoire 13
hit   frapper (*quelqu'un*) 43
HOBBIES   passe-temps 36-39
hold   tenir 54
HOMES   maisons 30-33
homework   devoirs (*à la maison*) 14
hop   sauter à cloche-pied 41
horse   cheval 25
horse riding   équitation 39
hospital   hôpital 46
hot   (très) chaud 59, 62
hot dog   hot-dog 28
hotel   hôtel 46
hour   heure (*60 minutes*) 57
house   maison 30

hovercraft   aéroglisseur 35
how   comment 34; how many   combien 10
hug   serrer dans les bras 43
hundred   cent 10
husband   mari 19

i

I   je 52
ice   glace (*eau gelée*) 62
ice cream   glace (*à manger*) 29
ice skating   patinage sur glace 39
if   si 40
igloo   igloo 7
imagine   imaginer 47
in   dans 60; dans, à 44; en 11, 22;
   in front of   devant 60
India   Inde 64
Indian   indien 64
insect   insecte 63
instruction   instruction 14
instrument   instrument 38
into   dans 60
Irish   irlandais 64
iron   fer à repasser 32; repasser 45
ironing board   planche à repasser 32
is   (*il, elle*) est 60
island   île 50
it   il, elle 60, 62
italian   italien(ne) 64
Italy   Italie 64

j

jacket   veste 20
jam   confiture 29
January   janvier 57
Japan   Japon 64
Japanese   japonais 64
jar   pot (*à confiture*) 7, 32
jeans   jean 20
jelly   gelée 29
jewellery   bijoux 21

jigsaw puzzle   puzzle 37
JOBS   métiers 52-53
judo   judo 39
jug   pot (à eau, etc) 60
juggle   jongler 43
juggler   jongleur 7
July   juillet 57
jump   sauter 41
jumper   pullover 20
June   juin 57

k

kangaroo   kangourou 23
kennel   niche 24
ketchup   ketchup 28
kettle   bouilloire 33
key   clef 7
kick   donner un coup de pied (à) 43
king   roi 55
kiss   embrasser 43
kitchen   cuisine (pièce) 32
kite   cerf-volant 7
kitten   petit chat 24
knee   genou 16
kneel   s'agenouiller 40
knickers   culotte (de femme) 20
knife   couteau 33
knit   tricoter 45
knock   frapper (à la porte) 43

l

label   étiqueter, marquer 16
ladder   échelle 7
ladybird   coccinelle 63
lake   lac 49
lamb   agneau 25
lamp   lampe 30
lamp-post   réverbère 47
land   tomber 40; terre 34
language   langue 31; language laboratory
   laboratoire de langues 12

large   grand, gros 58
laugh   rire 40
leaf   feuille 49
leaves   feuilles 49
leek   poireau 26
left   gauche 58
leg   patte 22; jambe 16
lemon   citron 27
lemonade   limonade 29
letter   lettre 7
lettuce   salade 27
library   bibliothèque (salle, bâtiment) 12
lifeguard   maître-nageur 51
lift   soulever 43
light   lumière 15; clair 59; léger 59
lighthouse   phare 50
lightning   éclair, éclairs 62
like   aimer 62
lime   citron vert 27
lion   lion 23
lip   lèvre 17
list   liste 8
listen (to)   écouter 45
litter   détritus 49
litter bin   poubelle 51
little   petit 58
live   vivre, habiter 22
living room   salle de séjour 33
lizard   lézard 23
lobster   homard 7
locust   criquet, grande sauterelle 63
long   long 58
longest   (le) plus long 7
look at   regarder 8
lorry   camion 35
loud   fort, bruyant 58
low   bas 59
lunch   déjeuner 13, 29

m

made of   en, fait de 8
magazine   magazine 50
magnet   aimant 7
make   faire 8
make-up   maquillage 37

man   homme 19
mango   mangue 27
mantis   mante 63
map   carte (*géographique*) 22
maracas   maraca 38
March   mars 57
market   marché 46
mask   masque 16
mat   carpette 61
match   allumette 7
material   matière 9
maths   maths 13
May   mai 57
meal   repas 29
mean   signifier, vouloir dire 58
measure   mesurer 43
meat   viande 29
mechanic   mécanicien 53
medal   médaille 37
melon   melon 26
mend   réparer 44
mermaid   sirène 55
metal   métal 9
Mexican   mexicain 64
Mexico   Mexique 64
mice   (des) souris 24
microwave   four micro-ondes 33
midday   midi 57
midnight   minuit 57
milk   lait 28
milkshake   milkshake 29
million   million 10
millipede   mille-pattes 63
mime   mimer 43
minibus   minibus 35
minute   minute 57
mirror   miroir 30
miss   manquer, perdre 40
model   modèle 37
Monday   lundi 56
money   argent (*que l'on dépense*) 37
money box   tirelire 37
monkey   singe 23
monster   monstre 18, 55
month   mois 57
moon   lune 55
mop   serpillière 33
more   autres, d'autres 19; plus 40
morning   matin, matinée 57

mosque   mosquée 46
mosquito   moustique 63
moth   papillon de nuit 63
mother   mère 18
motorbike   moto 35
motorway   autoroute 49
mountain   montagne 49
mouse   (une) souris 24
moustache   moustache 17
mouth   bouche 17
mouth organ   harmonica 38
move   déplacer 40
mug   grosse tasse 33
mum   maman 18
museum   musée 46
mushroom   champignon 26
music   musique 13, 38
mustard   moutarde 28
my   mon, ma, mes 12

n

name   nom 12
nationality   nationalité 64
near   près de 60
neck   cou 17
necklace   collier 21
need   avoir besoin de 40
needle   aiguille 7
nephew   neveu 19
nest   nid 49
Netherlands   Pays-Bas 64
new   nouveau, nouvelle 58
newspaper   journal (*d'actualités*) 7
New Zealand   Nouvelle-Zélande 64
New Zealander   Néo-Zélandais,
    Néo-Zélandaise 64
next to   à côté de 61
niece   nièce 18
night   nuit 57, 58
nightie   chemise de nuit 20
nine   neuf 10
nineteen   dix-neuf 10
ninety   quatre-vingt-dix 10
noisy   bruyant 58
north   nord 23

O

p

q

r

rocket   fusée 35
roller skate   patin à roulettes 35
roof   toit 30
room   salle, pièce 12, 36
rope   corde 7, 51
rough   rugueux 58
roundabout   carrousel 51
rubber   caoutchouc 9; gomme 13
rubber ring   bouée de natation 51
rubbish tip   décharge 49
rucksack   sac à dos 49
rug   carpette 30
rule   règle 40
ruler   règle 11, 13
run   courir 41
runway   piste d'envol 34

S

sad   triste 58
salad   salade 29
salt   sel 28
same   même, pareil 58
sand   sable 50
sand castle   château de sable 50
sandpit   tas de sable 51
sandwich   sandwich 29
satellite   satellite 34
Saturday   samedi 56
saucer   soucoupe 33
sausage   saucisse 29
saxophone   saxophone 38
say   dire 40
scales   balance 15
scar   cicatrice, balafre 17
scarecrow   épouvantail 49
scarf   écharpe 20
SCHOOL   école 12-15
science   science, sciences 13; science
    laboratory   laboratoire de sciences 12
scientist   savant 53
scissors   ciseaux 15
scooter   trottinette 35
scorpion   scorpion 63
scratch   gratter, se gratter 41
scream   crier (très fort) 41

sea   mer 34, 50
seal   phoque 23
seaside   bord de la mer 50
season   saison 57
seaweed   algue 50
second   deuxième 56; seconde 57
secretary   secrétaire 52
see   voir 8
seesaw   jeu de bascule 51
sentence   phrase 54
September   septembre 57
settee   canapé 33
seven   sept 10
seventeen   dix-sept 10
seventy   soixante-dix 10
sew   coudre 45
sewing machine   machine à coudre 33
shake   agiter 41
shape   forme 9
shark   requin 23
sharp   pointu 59
she   elle 43
sheep   mouton 25
sheet   feuille 50; drap 31
shelf   étagère 15
shell   coquillage 50
ship   navire 35
shirt   chemise 20
shoe   chaussure 20
shoelace   lacet 21
shop   magasin 47
shop assistant   vendeur, vendeuse 52
short   court 58; petit 58
shorts   short 20
shoulder   épaule 17
shout   crier 41
shower   douche 31
shut   fermé 59
signpost   poteau indicateur 49
silver   argenté 9
sing   chanter 41
singer   chanteur, chanteuse 52
sink   évier 33
sister   sœur 18
sit down   s'asseoir 41
six   six 10
sixteen   seize 10
sixty   soixante 10
skate   patiner 43

skateboard planche à roulettes 35	**square** carré 9; case 40
skeleton squelette 55	**staff room** salle des professeurs 12
ski skier 43	**stairs** escalier 32
skiing ski 39	**stamp** timbre-poste 37
skip sauter à la corde 43	**stand up** se lever 40
skipping rope corde à sauter 37	**stapler** agrafeuse 15
skirt jupe 20	**star** étoile 9
sky ciel 50	**starfish** étoile de mer 50
sleep dormir 45	**start** départ 40
slide toboggan 51	**stereo** chaîne stéréo 33
slipper pantoufle 20	**stick** coller 50; petit bâton 49
slow lent 59	**stick insect** phasme 63
slug limace 60	**sticky tape** scotch ® 15
small petit 58	**stomach** estomac 16
small letter minuscule 7	**stone** pierre 49
smile sourire 41	**stool** tabouret 33
smoke fumée 49	**stop** point 7
smooth lisse 58	**STORIES** histoires, contes 54-55
snail escargot 63	**storybook** livre de contes 55
snake serpent 23	**straight** raide 17
snorkel tuba 51	**strawberry** fraise 27
snow neige 62; neiger 62	**stream** ruisseau 49
snowman bonhomme de neige 7	**stretch** s'étirer 44
soap savon 31	**string** ficelle 15
sock chaussette 21	**strong** fort 58
sofa canapé 33	**stupid** stupide 59
soft doux, douce 58	**submarine** sous-marin 35
soft toy (jouet) peluche 37	**sugar** sucre 28
some des, quelques 19	**suitcase** valise 7
son fils 19	**summer** été 57
soup soupe 29	**sun** soleil 62
south sud 23	**Sunday** dimanche 56
space espace 8	**sunglasses** lunettes de soleil 50
space ship vaisseau spatial 35	**sunny** ensoleillé 62
space shuttle navette spatiale 35	**suntan lotion** crème solaire 50
spade pelle 50	**supermarket** supermarché 47
spaghetti spaghetti 29	**supper** repas du soir (léger) 29
Spain Espagne 64	**surfboard** planche de surf 50
Spanish espagnol 64	**sweater** pullover 20
speedboat hors-bord (bateau) 35	**sweatshirt** sweat-shirt 21
spell épeler 34	**Sweden** Suède 64
spelling orthographes 34	**Swedish** suédois 64
spider araignée 63	**sweep** balayer 44
spinach épinards 26	**sweet** bonbon 29
spoon cuiller 33	**swim** nager 43
sport sport 39	**swimming** natation 39
sports bag sac de sport 37	**swimming costume** maillot de bain 21
spring printemps 57	**swimming pool** piscine 51
sprout chou de Bruxelles 26	**swimming trunks** slip de bain 21

swing balançoire 51
Swiss Suisse 64
switch interrupteur 33
Switzerland Suisse 64
sword épée 55
synthesizer synthétiseur 38

t

table table 28, 33
tablecloth nappe 33
table tennis tennis de table 39
take prendre 43; take off enlever 44
tall grand 58
tambourine tambourin 38
tank char 35
tap robinet 31
tape cassette 15
taxi taxi 34
tea thé 28
teacher professeur, instituteur, institutrice 15
teapot théière 33
tear déchirer 43
teddy ours en peluche 37
teeth dents 16
telephone téléphone 33
telephone box cabine téléphonique 47
telescope téléscope 7
television télévision 33
ten dix 10
tennis tennis 39
tent tente 49
that qui 61
the le, la, les, l' 7
theatre théâtre 47
them les (objet d'un verbe) 31
then puis, ensuite 11
there là, là-bas 59; there is, there are il y a 61
these ces choses-ci 7; ces . . . -ci 11; ceux-ci, celles-ci 64
they ils, elles 43
thick épais 59
thin mince 59
thing chose 37
think of penser à 22
third troisième 56

thirteen treize 10
thirty trente 10
this ce . . .-ci, cette . . .-ci 7; ceci 40
thousand mille 10
three trois 10
throw lancer 43
thumb pouce 17
thunder tonnerre 62
Thursday jeudi 56
ticket billet 46
tie cravate 21; nouer 45
tiger tigre 23
tights collant 21
TIME heure 56-57; heure 29
timetable emploi du temps 13
to à 6
toast pain grillé 29
toaster grille-pain 33
today aujourd'hui 46
toe orteil 17
toilet toilettes 12; cuvette de W.C. 31
toilet paper papier hygiénique 31
tomato tomate 27
tongue langue 16
too aussi 25
tooth dent 16
toothbrush brosse à dents 31
toothpaste dentifrice 31
top haut 59
torch lampe de poche 37
tortoise tortue 7, 24
touch toucher 40
towel serviette de toilette 31
town ville 30, 46
town hall hôtel de ville 47
toy jouet 37
tracksuit survêtement 21
tractor tracteur 49
traffic lights feux de signalisation 47
train train 35; train set petit train (jouet) 37
trainer chaussure de sport 21
tram tramway 35
translate traduire 31
TRANSPORT moyens de transport 34-35
tray plateau 33
treasure trésor 55
tree arbre 49
triangle triangle 9, 38
tricycle tricycle 35

U

V

W

X

y

z

Français–Anglais

a

abeille bee 63
abricot apricot 26
acheter buy 43
à côte de by, next to 61
acteur (comédien) actor 52
actrice (comédienne) actress 52
adulte adult 19
aéroglisseur hovercraft 35
aéroport airport 46
affiche poster 15
Afrique Africa 23
agenda diary 37
agneau lamb 25
agrafeuse stapler 15
aiguille needle 7
aimant magnet 7
algue seaweed 50
Allemagne Germany 64
allemand German 64
allumer turn on 40
allumette match 7
alphabet alphabet 6-7
ambulance ambulance 35
américain American 64
Amérique America 23
an year 57
ananas pineapple 26
âne donkey 25
anglais English 13
animal animal 22-25
animal familier pet 24
Antarctique (l') Antarctica 23
antenne aerial 30
août August 57
appareil-photo camera 37
appartement flat 30
après-midi afternoon 57
araignée spider 63
arbre tree 49
arc-en-ciel rainbow 7
argent (*que l'on dépense*) money 37
argenté silver 9

argentin Argentinian 64
Argentine Argentina 64
armoire wardrobe 31
arrêt d'autobus bus stop 47
arrière back 58
artiste artist 52
Asie Asia 23
asperges asparagus 27
aspirateur vacuum cleaner 33
asseoir (s'asseoir) sit down 41
assiette plate 33
astronaute astronaut 7
athlétisme athletics 39
attraper catch 43
aubergine aubergine 27
au-dessus de above 60
Australasie Australasia 23
Australie Australia 64
australien Australian 64
autobus bus 35
autographe autograph 37
automne autumn 57
autoroute motorway 49
Autriche Austria 64
autrichien Austrian 64
autruche ostrich 23
avant (*l'avant d'un véhicule, etc*) front 58
avion aeroplane, plane 35
avocat (*légume*) avocado 27
avril April 57

b

badge badge 11, 37
bague ring 21
baguette magique wand 55
baignoire bath 30
bâiller yawn 45
baladeur personal stereo 37
balafre scar 16
balai brush 7; broom 61
balance scales 15
balançoire swing 51
balayer sweep 44
balcon balcony 30
baleine whale 23

balle ball 37
ballon balloon 7
banane banana 26
banc bench 51
banjo banjo 38
banque bank 47
barbe beard 16
barrette hair slide 21
bas bottom 59; low 59; en bas down 60;
  downstairs 32
bascule jeu de bascule seesaw 51
base-ball baseball 39
basket-ball basketball 39
bâton; petit bâton stick 49
bateau boat 35
bâtiment building 46
bâtir build 43
batte bat 37
battre des mains clap 40
beau beautiful 58
bébé baby 19
beignet doughnut 28
belge Belgian 64
Belgique Belgium 64
bête animal 22–25
betterave beetroot 27
beurre butter 29
bibliothèque bookcase 15; library 12
bicyclette bicycle 35
bière beer 28
bijoux jewellery 21
bikini bikini 20
biscuit biscuit 28
blanc, blanche white 9
blé (maïs) corn 26
bleu blue 9
blond blonde, fair 17
bœuf beef 29
boire drink 44
bois wood 9
boisson drink 28
boîte box 15
boîte aux lettres postbox 47
bol bowl 33
bon right 58
bonbon sweet 29
bonhomme de neige snowman 7
bon marché cheap 59
bord de la mer seaside 50

botte boot 20
bouche mouth 16
bouchon plug 30
bouclé curly 17
boucle d'oreille earring 21
bouée de natation rubber ring 55; bouée pour
  les bras armband 32
bougie candle 7
bouilloire kettle 33
boule ball 11
bouteille bottle 32
bouton button 21
bracelet bracelet 21
bras arm 16
Brésil Brazil 64
brésilien Brazilian 64
britannique British 64
brocoli broccoli 27
brosse brush 7; brosse à cheveux hairbrush
  37; brosse à dents toothbrush 31; brosse à
  tableau board rubber 15
brouette wheelbarrow 51
brouillard fog 62
brumeux foggy 62
brun brown 9; dark 17
bruyant noisy 58
buisson bush 49
bureau office 12; desk 15

C

cabine téléphonique telephone box 47
cacher (se cacher) hide 43
cafard cockroach 63
café (*café-restaurant*) cafe 46
café (*à boire*) coffee 28
cage cage 7
cage à poules climbing frame 51
cahier (petit cahier) notebook 13
calculatrice calculator 11,15
calendrier calendar 56
camion lorry, truck 35
camionnette van 35
campagne countryside 48
camping (*endroit*) campsite 20
Canada Canada 64

canadien   Canadian 64
canal   canal 49
canapé   settee, sofa 33
canard   duck 25
canne   stick 49
canne à pêche   fishing rod 51
canoë   canoe 35
caoutchouc   rubber 9
car   coach 35
caravane   caravan 35
carnet   notebook 13
carotte   carrot 27
carpette   rug 30; mat 61
carré   square 9
carrousel   roundabout 51
carte à jouer   playing card 11
carte   card 37
carte postale   postcard 37
case   square 40
casque à écouteurs   headphones 37
casserole   pan 33
casser   break 44
cassette   cassette, tape 15
caverne   cave 49
ceinture   belt 21
céleri   celery 26
cent   a hundred 10
centrale électrique   power station 49
cercle   circle 9
céréale   cereal 15
cerf-volant   kite 7
cerise   cherry 26
chaîne stéréo   stereo 33
chaise   chair 15
chaland   barge 35
chambre (à coucher)   bedroom 31
chameau   camel 23
champ   field 49
champignon   mushroom 27
chanter   sing 41
chanteur (chanteuse)   singer 52
chapeau   hat 20
char   tank 35
chat   cat 24; petit chat   kitten 24
château   castle 55; château de sable   sandcastle 50
chaud (assez chaud)   warm 62; (très chaud) hot 59, 62
chaussette   sock 21

chaussure   shoe 20; chaussure de sport   traine
21; chaussure de football   football boot 37
chauve   bald 17
chauve-souris   bat 23
chef de cuisine   chef 53
cheminée (sur le toit)   chimney 30
chemise   shirt 20; chemise de nuit   nightie 20
chenille   caterpillar 63
cher   expensive, dear; pas cher   cheap 59
cheval   horse 25
chevalet   easel 15
cheveux   hair 16
cheville   ankle 16
chèvre   goat 25
chez soi   home, at home 30–35
chien   dog 24; jeune chien   puppy 24
Chili   Chile 64
chilien   Chilean 64
chip   crisp 28
chocolat   chocolate 28
chose   thing 37
chou   cabbage 27
chou de Bruxelles   sprout 37
chou-fleur   cauliflower 26
chuchoter   whisper 41
chute d'eau   waterfall 49
cicatrice   scar 16
ciel   sky 50
cigale   cicada 63
cil   eyelash 16
cinéma   cinema 46
cinq   five 10
cinquante   fifty 10
cirque   circus 36
ciseaux   scissors 15
citron   lemon 26
citron vert   lime 26
clair   light 59
clarinette   clarinet 38
classe   class 13; salle de classe   classroom 12
classeur   file 15
clef   key 7
cloporte   woodlouse 63
clôture   fence 49
clown   clown 37
coca ®   cola 28
coccinelle   ladybird 63
cochon   pig 25; petit cochon   piglet 25
cochon d'Inde   guinea pig 24

cœur heart 9
coiffeur (coiffeuse) hairdresser 53
collant tights 21
collation (*avant de se coucher*) supper 29
colle glue 15
collectionner collect 37
collier necklace 21
colline hill 49
compas compass 15
concombre cucumber 27
conducteur d'autobus bus driver 53
conduire drive 43
confiture jam 29
congélateur freezer 32
contraire OPPOSITE 58-59
contrebasse double bass 38
copier copy 43
coq cockerel 25
coquillage shell 50
corbeille à papier bin 15
corde rope 7,51
corde à sauter skipping rope 37
corps body 16-17; torse body 16
côté; à côté de next to 61
cou neck 16
coude elbow 16
coudre sew 45
couette duvet 30
couleur colour 8-9
couleurs paints 37
coup; donner un coup de pied à kick 43
couper cut 45
cour de récréation playground 12,42
courgette courgette 27
courir run 41
couronne crown 55
court short 58
cousin cousin 18
coussin cushion 32
couteau knife 33
couverture blanket 30
crabe crab 50
craie chalk 15
cravate tie 7, 21
crayon pencil 13
crayon de couleur crayon 13
creuser dig 43
cricket cricket 39
cri-cri cricket; gros cri-cri cicada 63

crier shout 41; (*très fort*) scream 41
criquet locust 63
crocodile crocodile 23
croissant croissant 29
cube brick 37
cuiller spoon 33
cuire; faire cuire cook 45
cuisine kitchen 32
cuisinière cooker 32
culotte (*de femme*) knickers 20
cuvette de W.C. toilet 31
cymbale cymbal 38

d

Danemark Denmark 64
danois Danish 64
dans in 60
danser dance 41
danseur (danseuse) dancer 53
dauphin dolphin 23
dé dice 11
décembre December 57
décharge rubbish tip 49
déchirer tear 43
dehors outside 30
déjeuner lunch 13, 29; petit déjeuner
   breakfast 29
deltaplane hang glider 35
demi half 11; et demi half past 57
dent (dents) tooth (teeth) 16
dentifrice toothpaste 31
dentiste dentist 53
départ start 40
derrière bottom 16; derrière behind 60
dessin (image) drawing 15
dessiner draw 41
détritus litter 49
deux two 10
deuxième second 56
devant in front of 60
devoirs (*à la maison*) homework 14
différent different 58
difficile difficult 59
dimanche Sunday 56
dîner dinner 29

dinosaure   dinosaur 7
diplomate   trifle 29
dirigeable   airship 35
dix   ten 10
dix-huit   eighteen 10
dix-neuf   nineteen 10
dix-sept   seventeen 10
djinn   genie 55
docteur   doctor 52
doigt   finger 16
doigt de pied   toe 16
domino   domino 11
donner   give 43
dormir   sleep 44
dos   back 16
douche   shower 31
doux (douce)   soft 58
douze   twelve 10
dragon   dragon 55
drap   sheet 31
drapeau   flag 7,64
droit   right 58
dur   hard 58, 59

eau   water 28, 51
écharpe   scarf 20
échelle   ladder 7
éclair (éclairs)   lightning 62
école   school 12-15
écouter   listen (to) 44
écouteurs   headphones 37
écrire   write 41
éducation physique   physical education 13
église   church 46
électricien   electrician 52
éléphant   elephant 23
élève   pupil 15
embrasser   kiss 43
emploi du temps   timetable 13
employé(e) de banque   bank clerk 52
en avant   forward 40
endroit   place 46-51
enfant   child; enfants   children 19
enlever   take off 45

ensoleillé   sunny 62
entre   between 60
entrée   entrance 12
enveloppe   envelope 7
épais   thick 59
épaule   shoulder 16
épée   sword 55
épinards   spinach 27
épingle   pin 7
épointé   blunt 59
épouvantail   scarecrow 49
équitation   horse riding 39
escalier   stairs 32
escargot   snail 63
espace   space 8
Espagne   Spain 64
espagnol   Spanish 64
est   east 23
estomac   stomach 16
étage; au premier étage   upstairs 30
étagère   shelf 15
étang   pond 51
États-Unis   U.S.A 64
été   summer 57
éteindre   turn off 40
étirer (s'étirer)   stretch 44
étoile   star 9
étoile de mer   starfish 50
Europe   Europe 23
évier   sink 33
extra-terrestre   alien 55

facile   easy 59
facteur   postman 53
faible   weak 58; quiet 58
falaise   cliff 50
famille   family 18-19
fantôme   ghost 55
fauteuil   armchair 32; fauteuil
   roulant   wheelchair 35
faux (fausse)   wrong 59
fée   fairy 55
femme   wife, woman 19
femme-agent   policewoman 53

fenêtre window 14
fer à repasser iron 32
fermé closed 47, 59
ferme farm 25; farmhouse 49
fermer close, shut 41
fermeture éclair ® zip 7
ferry ferry 35
fête party 28
feu fire 49
feuille (feuilles) leaf (leaves) 49
feux de signalisation traffic lights 47
février February 57
ficelle string 15
fille daughter 18; girl 19
film film 46
fils son 19
finlandais Finnish 64
Finlande Finland 64
flaque puddle 62
fleur flower 51
fleuve river 49
flûte flute 38
flûte à bec recorder 38
fois; il était une fois once upon a time 54
fontaine fountain 51
football football 39
forêt forest 49
forme shape 9
fort strong 58; loud 58
four oven 33
four micro-ondes microwave 33
fourchette fork 33
fourmi ant 63
fraction fraction 11
fraise strawberry 26
framboise raspberry 27
français French 64
France France 64
frapper (quelqu'un) hit 43; (à la porte) knock 43
frère brother 18
frigo fridge 32
frise curly 17
frite chip 29
froid cold 59, 62
fromage cheese 29
front forehead 16
fruit (fruits) fruit 26
fumée smoke 49
fusée rocket 35

fusée de feu d'artifice firework 7

g

galet pebble 50
gant glove 20
garage garage 30
garçon boy 19
gare railway station 47
gâteau; petit gâteau sec biscuit 28; gâteau d'anniversaire birthday cake 28
gauche left 58
géant giant 55
gelée jelly 29
genou knee 16
gens people 19
géographie geography 13
gilet cardigan 30
girafe giraffe 23
glace ice cream 29; ice 62
golf golf 39
gomme rubber 13
gorille gorilla 23
grand big, tall 58
grand-mère grandmother 18
grands-parents grandparents 18
grand-père grandfather 18
grange barn 49
gras (grasse) fat 59
gratter (se gratter) scratch 41
grec (grecque) Greek 64
Grèce Greece 64
grenouille frog 24
grille-pain toaster 33
grillon cricket 63
grimper (sur) climb 43
gris grey 9
gros (grosse) big, large 58; fat 59
guêpe wasp 63
guitare guitar 38
gymnase gymnasium, gym 12
gymnastique gymnastics 39

h

habiller (s'habiller) get dressed 45
habile (intelligent) clever 59
hache axe 55
hall d'entrée hallway 32
hamac hammock 49
hamburger hamburger 28
hamburger au fromage cheeseburger 28
hamster hamster 24
haricot bean 26
harmonica mouth organ 38
harpe harp 38
haut high, top 59
hélicoptère helicopter 35
herbe grass 49
hérisson hedgehog 23
heure time 29; l'heure qu'il est time 56–57;
 (60 minutes) hour 57
heureux happy 58
hibou owl 23
hippopotame hippopotamus 23
histoire story 54-55; history 13
hiver winter 57
hollandais Dutch 64
homard lobster 7
homme man 19
hôpital hospital 46
horloge clock 15
hors de out of 61
hors-bord speedboat 35
hot-dog hot dog 28
hôtel hotel 47
hôtel de ville town hall 47
huit eight 10

i

ici here 59
igloo igloo 7
île island 50
immeuble (de résidence) flats 30; immeuble (*de bureaux*) office-building 47

Inde India 64
indien Indian 64
infirmière nurse 52
instrument instrument 38
intelligence clever 49
interrupteur switch 33
irlandais Irish 64
Irlande; République d'Irlande Eire 64
Italie Italy 64

j

jambe leg 16
jambon ham 29
janvier January 57
Japon Japan 64
japonais Japanese 64
jardin garden 30
jaune yellow 9
jean jeans 20
jeu game 37
jeu électronique computer game 37
jeu de société board game 40
jeudi Thursday 56
jeune young 59
jongler juggle 43
jongleur juggler 7
joue cheek 16
jouet toy 37
jour day 57, 58
journal newspaper 7
judo judo 39
juillet July 57
juin June 57
jupe skirt 20
jus de fruit fruit juice 28
juste right 58

k

kangourou kangaroo 23
ketchup ketchup 28

l

là (*là-bas*)   there 59
laboratoire de langues   language laboratory 12
laboratoire de sciences   science laboratory 12
lac   lake 49
lacet   shoelace 21
laid   ugly 58
laine   wool 9
lait   milk 28
lampe   lamp 30
lampe de poche   torch 37
lancer   throw 43
langue   tongue 16
lapin   rabbit 24
lard   bacon 29
lavabo   wash basin 41
lave-vaisselle   dishwasher 32
laver (*se laver*)   wash 44
léger   light 59
légume   vegetable 26
lent   slow 59
lettre   letter 7
lever   lift 43; se lever   stand-up 40; get up 44
lèvre   lip 16
lézard   lizard 23
libellule   dragonfly 63
lièvre   hare 61
limace   slug 60
limonade   lemonade 29
lion   lion 23
lire   read 41
lisse   smooth 58
lit   bed 30
livre   book 37
long   long 58
lotion solaire   suntan lotion 50
loup   wolf 23
lourd   heavy 59
luciole   firefly 63
lumière   light 15
lundi   Monday 56
lune   moon 55
lunettes   glasses 21; lunettes de plongée   goggles 51; lunettes de soleil   sunglasses 50

m

machine; machine à coudre   sewing machine 33; machine à écrire   typewriter 37; machine à laver   washing machine 33
maçon   builder 52
magasin   shop 47; magasin de bandes dessinées   comic shop 37
magicien   wizard 55
magnétoscope   video 15
mai   May 57
maillot de bain   swimming costume 21
maillot de corps   vest 21
main   hand 16; faire signe de la main   wave 41
mais   corn 26
maison   house 30; home 30-33; petite maison à la campagne   cottage 55
maison de poupée   doll's house 37
maître-nageur   lifeguard 51
majuscule   capital 7
maman   mum 18
manche à balai   broomstick 55
manger   eat 45
mangue   mango 27
mante   mantis 63
manteau   coat 20
maquillage   make-up 37
maraca   maracas 38
marché   market 47
marcher   walk 40; marcher à quatre pattes   crawl 41
mardi   Tuesday 56
mari   husband 19
marionnette   puppet 16
mars   March 57
marteau   hammer 7
masque   mask 16
maths   maths 13
matière   material 9
matin (*matinée*)   morning 57
mécanicien   mechanic 53
méchant   bad 58
médaille   medal 37
melon   melon 27
même   same 38
menton   chin 16

mer sea 34,50
mercredi Wednesday 56
mère mother 18
mesurer measure 43
métal metal 9
métier job 52-53
mettre (*un vêtement*) put on 45
meule de foin haystack 49
mexicain Mexican 64
Mexique Mexico 64
midi midday 57
milkshake milkshake 39
mille a thousand 10
mille-pattes centipede, millipede 63
million million 10
mince thin 59
minibus minibus 35
minuit midnight 57
minuscule small 7
minute minute 57
miroir mirror 30
modèle model 37
mois month 57
monstre monster 18,55
montagne mountain 49
monter à ride 43
montgolfière balloon 35
montre watch 37
montrer du doigt point 40
mordre bite 43
mort dead 58
mosquée mosque 47
mot word 7
moto motorbike 35
mouche fly 63
mouillé wet 59
moustache moustache 16
moustique mosquito 63
moutarde mustard 28
mouton sheep 25
mur wall 14
musée museum 47
musique music 13, 38

n

nager swim 43
nappe table cloth 33
natation swimming 39
navet turnip 37
navette spatiale space shuttle 35
navire ship 35
neige snow 62
neiger snow 62
Néo-Zélandais (Néo-Zélandaise) New Zealander 64
nettoyer clean 44
neuf nine 10
neveu nephew 19
nez nose 16
nid nest 49
nièce niece 18
noir black 9
noisette noix nut 29
noix de coco coconut 26
nord north 23
Norvège Norway 64
norvégien Norwegian 64
nouer tie 45
nourriture food 26-29
nouveau, nouvelle new 58
Nouvelle-Zélande New Zealand 64
novembre November 57
nuage cloud 62
nuageux cloudy 62
nuit night 57, 58
numéro number 10-11

o

obscur dark 59
octobre October 57
oeil eye 16
œuf egg 29
oie goose 25
oignon onion 27
oiseau bird 60
oncle uncle 18

onze   eleven 10
or (couleur or)   gold 9
orange   orange 26
orangé   orange 9
ordinateur   computer 15
oreille   ear 16
oreiller   pillow 30
ouest   west 23
ours   bear 23
ours en peluche   teddy 57
ouvert   open 46, 59
ouvrir   open 40

pain   bread 29
pain grillé   toast 39
palais   palace 55
palme   flipper 51
pamplemousse   grapefruit 26
panda   panda 23
panneau d'affichage   noticeboard 13
panneau routier   road sign 47
pantalon   trousers 21
pantoufle   slipper 20
papa   dad 18
papaye   papaya 27
papier   paper 9, 15
papier hygiénique   toilet paper 31
papillon   butterfly 63
papillon de nuit   moth 63
parachute   parachute 35
parapluie   umbrella 7
parc   park 51
par-dessus (sur)   over 61
parent   parent 18
parking   car park 46
passage pour piétons   pedestrian crossing 47
pastèque   watermelon 27
patin à roulettes   roller skate 35
patinage sur glace   ice skating 39
patiner   skate 43
pauvre   poor 59
Pays-Bas (les)   The Netherlands 64
pêche   peach 26
pêcher   fish 43

peigne   comb 37
peigner   comb 44
peindre   paint 43
peler   peel 44
pélican   pelican 23
peluche (jouet)   soft toy 37
pelle   spade 50
pendule   clock 11
péniche   barge 35
perce-oreille   earwig 15
père   father 18
Pérou   Peru 64
perroquet   parrot 24
perruche   budgie 24
personnage   character 55
personne (*personnes*)   person (*people*) 19
personnel   personal 37
péruvien   Peruvian 64
peser   weigh 44
petit   small, short, little 58
petit-fille   granddaughter 18
petit-fils   grandson 19
petit pois   pea 26
phare   lighthouse 50
phasme   stick insect 63
phoque   seal 23
piano   piano 38
pièce   room 36
pièce d'eau   pond 51
pièce de monnaie   coin 37
pied (pieds)   foot (feet) 16
pierre   stone 49
pieuvre   octopus 7,23
pilote   pilot 52
pinceau   paint brush 15
pingouin   penguin 23
pique-nique   picnic 49
pirate   pirate 55
piscine   swimming pool 51
pistolet   gun 37
pizza   pizza 39
placard   cupboard 15
plafond   ceiling 14
plage   beach 50
planche; planche à repasser   ironing board 32
   planche à roulettes   skateboard 35 planche de
   surf   surfboard 50
plancher   floor 15
plante   plant 15

plastique   plastic 9
plat   dish 60
plateau   tray 33
plein   full 59
pleurer   cry 41
pleuvoir   rain 62
plombier   plumber 52
plongeoir   diving board 51
plonger   dive 43
pluie   rain 62
plume   feather 50
pluvieux   wet 59, 62
poche   pocket 21
point   full stop 7
point d'interrogation   question mark 7
pointu   sharp 59
poire   pear 26
poireau   leek 26
poisson   fish 24, 29
poitrine   chest 16
poivre   pepper 28
poivron   pepper 26
pomme   apple 26
pomme de terre   potato 27
pompier   fireman 52
ponctuation   punctuation 7
pont   bridge 49
porte   door 14; gate 49
porte-monnaie   purse 37
porter   carry 43
portugais   Portuguese 64
Portugal   Portugal 64
position   position 60-61
poste; bureau de poste   post office 47
poste de police   police station 47
pot à confitures   jar 7,32
pot   jug 60
poteau indicateur   signpost 49
poubelle   dustbin 7; litter bin 51
pouce   thumb 16
poule   hen 25
poulet   chicken 29
poupée   doll 37
pousser   push 43
poussette   pushchair 35
poussin   chick 25
premier   first 56
prendre   take 43; have   44
près de   near 60

prince   prince 55
princesse   princess 55
printemps   spring 57
prise   plug 33
professeur   teacher 15
propre   clean 59
prune   plum 27
puce   flea 63
pullover   jumper, sweater 20
punaise   drawing pin 15
pupitre   desk 15
puzzle   jigsaw puzzle 37
pyjama   pyjamas 30
pylône   pylon 49

q

quand   when 52
quarante   forty 10
quart   quarter 11; . . . et quart   quarter past 57;
   moins le quart   quarter to . . . 57
quatorze   fourteen 10
quatre   four 10
quatre-vingt-dix   ninety 10
quatre-vingts   eighty 10
quatrième   fourth 56
quinze   fifteen 10

r

raide   straight 17
raisin   grape 26
ramasser   pick up 40
rapide   fast 59
rat   rat 24
rayon   shelf 15
rebondir (faire rebondir)   bounce 43
récréation   break 13
rectangle   rectangle 9
regarder   watch 45
règle   ruler 11,13
reine   queen 7,55
renard   fox 23

réparer   mend 44
repas   meal 29
repasser   iron 45
requin   shark 23
réservoir   reservoir 49
restaurant   restaurant 47
retour; de retour, en retour   back 41
rêver   dream 44
réverbère   lamp post 47
rez-de-chaussée   downstairs 32
rhinocéros   rhinoceros 23
riche   rich 59
rideau   curtain 30
rire   laugh 40
rivière   river 49
riz   rice 29
robe   dress 20
robe de chambre   dressing gown 20
robinet   tap 31
robot   robot 37
rocher   rock 50
roi   king 55
rose   pink 9
roue   wheel 7
rouge   red 9
route   road 47
roux (rousse)   ginger 17
Royaume-Uni (le)   U.K. 64
ruban   ribbon 21
rue   road 47
rugueux   rough 58
ruisseau   stream 49

S

sable   sand 50
sac   bag 13
sac à dos   rucksack 49
sac à main   handbag 37
sac de sport   sports bag 37
saison   season 57
salade   salad 39; lettuce 26
sale   dirty 59
salle   room 12
salle (grande salle)   hall 12
salle de bains   bathroom 30

salle à manger   dining room 33
salle des professeurs   staff room 12
salle de séjour   living room 33
samedi   Saturday 56
sandwich   sandwich 39
saucisse   sausage 29
sauter   jump 41
sauter à cloche-pied   hop 41
sauter à la corde   skip 43
sauterelle   grasshopper 7, 63; grande
  sauterelle   locust 63
savant   scientist 53
savon   soap 31
saxophone   saxophone 38
scarabée   beetle 63
science   science 13
scooter   scooter 35
scorpion   scorpion 63
scotch ®   sticky tape 15
seau   bucket 50
sec (sèche)   dry 59
sèche-cheveux   hairdryer 37
sécher   dry 44
seconde   second 57
secrétaire   secretary 52
seize   sixteen 10
sel   salt 28
semaine   week 57
sept   seven 10
septembre   September 57
serpillière   mop 33
serpent   snake 23
serrer (*dans les bras*)   hug 43
serveur   waiter 53
serveuse   waitress 53
serviette de toilette   towel 31
short   shorts 20
siffler   whistle 41
singe   monkey 23
sirène   mermaid 55
six   six 10
ski   skiing 39
skier   ski 43
slip (*pour hommes*)   underpants 21
slip de bain   swimming trunks 21
sœur   sister 18
soir (soirée)   evening 57
soixante   sixty 10
soixante-dix   seventy 10

soleil   sun 62
sonnerie   bell 15
sont   are 60
sorcière   witch 55
sortie   exit 46
soucoupe   saucer 33
souffler   blow 40
soulever   lift 43
soupe (potage)   soup 29
sourcil   eyebrow 16
sourire   smile 41
souris (des souris)   mouse (mice) 24
sous   under 61
sous-marin   submarine 35
soutien-gorge   bra 20
spaghetti   spaghetti 29
sparadrap   plaster 7
sport   sport 39
squelette   skeleton 55
station-service   petrol station 47
store   blind 32
stupide   stupid 59
stylo   pen 13
sucre   sugar 28
sud   South 23
Suède   Sweden 64
suédois   Swedish 64
suisse   Swiss 64
Suisse (pays)   Switzerland 64
supermarché   supermarket 47
sur   on, over 61
survêtement   tracksuit 21
sweat-shirt   sweatshirt 21
synthétiseur   synthesizer 38

table   table 28,33
tableau   picture 30
tableau blanc   whiteboard 15
tableau noir   blackboard 15
tabouret   stool 33
tache de rousseur   freckle 16
taille-crayon   pencil sharpener 13
talkie-walkie   walkie talkie 37
tambour   drum 38

tambourin   tambourine 38
tante   aunt 18
tapis   carpet 30
tas de sable   sand pit 51
tasse   cup 33; grosse tasse   mug 33
taureau   bull 25
taxi   taxi 34
tee-shirt   t-shirt 21
télé   TV 33
téléphone   telephone 33
téléscope   telescope 7
télévision   television 33
temps   weather 62
tennis   tennis 39
tennis de table   table tennis 39
tente   tent 49
terre   land 34
tête   head 16
thé   tea 28
théâtre   theatre 47
théière   teapot 33
tigre   tiger 23
timbre-poste   stamp 37
tirelire   money box 37
tirer   pull 43
tiroir   drawer 15
tissu   cloth 9
toboggan   slide 51
toile d'araignée   cobweb 7
toilettes   toilet 12
toit   roof 30
tomate   tomato 26
tomber   fall 41; laisser tomber   drop 41
tonnerre   thunder 62
tortue   tortoise 7, 24
tortue de mer   turtle 23
toucher   touch 40
tour   turn 40
tousser   cough 41
tracteur   tractor 49
train   train 35
train (de jeu)   train set 37
tramway   tram 35
transat   deckchair 50
transport   transport 34–35
treize   thirteen 10
trente   thirty 10
trésor   treasure 55
triangle   triangle 9, 38

u

V

W, X

y, z